THE CHRISTIANITY OF JESUS

R. H. Backwell

VOLTURNA PRESS

THIS BOOK IS DEDICATED TO
Hasan Balyuzi, Evelyn Baxter,
Dorothy Cansdale, John Ferraby
and Isobel Slade
who set me on a new path in 1942

First Published in 1972

by

Volturna Press,
Wellington Place,
Peterhead,
Scotland.
ISBN 0 85606 019 4

Second printing 1973

Printed by
Bideford Gazette Ltd.,
5, Grenville Street,
Bideford.

THE CHRISTIANITY OF JESUS

THE CHRISTIANITY OF JESUS

FOREWORD

There seems to be an ever-growing need in this age for a simple, factual presentation of the Life and Teaching of Jesus, to enable all those who value that sublime Being to re-assure themselves that true Christianity, freed from all irrational and superstitious elements, constitutes an unchallengeable foundation for faith, and a matchless influence for the good of human kind.

" If two people dispute about religion, both are wrong."

The keen scalpel of these words will of itself help to cut back to the original story through the coccooning bands of mummy cloth that have wrapped it up for so long.

There are, basically, only four ways in which the subject of Christianity, or indeed of any revealed religion, can be viewed, the viewpoint depending on the condition or station of the viewer:—

1. The viewer may be totally immersed in worldly matters, indifferent to anything spiritual. He will then be like a light burning in a closed or shuttered room able only to obtain illumination from the reflection of his own light on the dark walls of the claustral environment, like a glow-worm which finds itself caught in a rabbit warren with the entrance blocked.

2. The viewer may be outside in the open and may be wearing tinted spectacles which he is afraid to remove because those who gave them to him have persuaded him that he would be blinded and lost if he took them off.

3. The viewer may be looking in such a way that although he is out in the open and not wearing tinted spectacles, he can see only the rays of the sun; he is overwhelmed by their brilliance and looks only at them.

4. The viewer may be looking at the sun itself—a perfectly safe thing to do until the sun rises too high above the horizon.

These four kinds of viewers typify everyone we know. The first is the materialist, or atheist, who is indifferent to, or denies the existence of the sun because the sun never reaches him. The second is the member of a Church, each Church providing a different colour to the spectacles, or he may be of a different religion. The third is the mystic who is free from denominational limitation but yet mistakes the effulgence which illumines his ego for the centre point of authority and progressive development. Only the fourth has a clear view.

Let us now look at that Sun of Truth. Jesus said: " I am the door of the sheep "[1]. " He that entereth not by the door into the sheepfold, but climbeth up some other way, the same is a thief and a robber." [2]. Too long has Christianity suffered from " thieves and robbers ".

Chapter 1

LIFE OF JESUS

" Glorified are Thou, O Lord my God! My tongue, both the tongue of my body and the tongue of my heart, my limbs and members, every pulsating vein within me, every hair of my head, all proclaim that Thou art God, and that there is none other God beside Thee. From everlasting Thou has been immeasurably exalted above all similitudes and comparisons, and sanctified from whatsoever pertaineth to the creation Thou hast created and fashioned. From eternity Thou hast been alone, with none to share the majesty of Thy singleness, and has remained far above the changes and chances to which all Thy creatures are subjected.

" And when Thou didst purpose to demonstrate the power of Thy sovereign might, and to glorify Thy word, and to guide the steps of Thy people, Thou didst raise up from among Thy creatures One of Thy servants, Whom Thou didst endow with the clear tokens of Thy oneness, that He might fulfil Thy testimony unto all created things, and perfect Thy proof before all men."[1]

Birth and early years

Jesus was born of Mary, who at that time was engaged to be married to Joseph, direct descendant of David and of Abraham, on a day and in a year not yet determined with complete certainty, between 1965 and 1975 solar years ago. He was the eldest of several children, including four brothers and some sisters, later born of the union of Mary and Joseph.

Joseph was of the tribe of Judah and lived in Nazareth, about 65 miles to the north of Jerusalem, where he pursued his trade as a carpenter, a trade to which he later apprenticed his oldest son.

At the time when Mary's first pregnancy was far advanced a decree was issued by Augustus Caesar, who at that time held power in Rome, for a census or general registration to be taken throughout the territories over which Rome held sway. These territories included Judaea and Galilee in which Jerusalem and Nazareth are located. For the purpose of the registration everyone was to go to his proper place, his own home town. Joseph therefore went to Judaea to be registered at Bethlehem, the city home of the royal line of David to which he belonged. So it was at Bethlehem, some 6 miles to the south of Jerusalem, that Jesus was born, in a manger or animal feeding trough because there was no room at the inn.

The child was circumcised eight days after birth in accordance with Jewish law, and taken by His parents to Jerusalem to be dedicated to the Lord God of Israel, and for the statutory offering of turtle doves and pigeons to be made.

Certain astrologers, probably followers of Zoroaster from Chaldea, arrived in Jerusalem and warned Herod, ruler of the province of Judaea at that time, that One was being born then Who was destined to become the King of the Jews. Herod, in fear for his authority, ordered the massacre of all babies in Bethlehem who were under two years of age. Joseph and Mary, forewarned, fled with their Baby to Egypt, where they remained until Herod had died and it was safe to return, but instead of Bethlehem or Jerusalem, they settled again at Nazareth near the Sea of Galilee.

When Jesus was twelve years old His parents took Him with them for their annual visit to Jerusalem for the feast of the Passover, which commemorated the passing over Jewish homes by the avenging angel who put to death the first-born of all Egyptian families, an event that led directly to the freedom of the Jews from the Pharaohs some 1300 or 1400 years earlier. When Joseph and Mary set off to return home after the feast, Jesus could not be found. Eventually they discovered Him sitting in the Temple discoursing intelligently with the religious teachers.

Commencement of Mission

When Jesus was about thirty years old, one John (Yahya), son of Zachariah and Elizabeth and slightly older than Jesus, was called by God to arise as a prophet in the wilderness, summon the people to repent of their backslidings and disobedience to the law of Moses, and to baptise those who so repented. Jesus too, in His great humility, went down to the river Jordan in which the people were baptised and was Himself baptised by John. John the Baptist is the name that was given to this great forerunner of Jesus. As so often happens to the great ones of the earth, he was thrown into prison and later beheaded by Herod (not to be confused with the other Herod) ruler of Galilee, for daring to warn and criticise in public the depraved members of Herod's household.

As Jesus came up from the river after His baptism He experienced an awakening call to His great mission, and felt impelled into the desert for forty days and forty nights, withdrawn from society to meditate and commune with God concerning that mission.

On return from the desert, Jesus first proclaimed His message, of the near approach of the kingdom of God, in the synagogues, or Jewish meeting houses, of Nazareth and Capernaum in the Galilee area, and then in the synagogues of Judaea. The congregations either ignored Him or turned against Him because of His trenchant challenge. Jesus therefore turned his attention to the underprivileged, the diseased and the poor, who responded to His authoritative sweet reasonableness by giving Him a hearing in ever increasing numbers.

Call to Disciples

As He went round expounding His message to all who would
listen, He chose twelve receptive souls in quick succession, starting
with a fisherman named Simon, later called Peter. They were to
leave their present activities and follow Him round wherever He
went. He continued to associate with poor people and people who
were socially disdained, even prostitutes, and among them lived
an active life enjoying His food and drink as much as His company.
He even broke the Sabbath and encouraged His disciples to do the
same. As time went by He was joined by a number of women
including especially Mary of Magdala, a well known prostitute.
With His immediate followers He travelled widely and ever larger
crowds turned out to meet Him and hear what He had to say.
He also engaged in private discussions with His disciples helping
them to overcome their handicaps of poor education and understanding. He even sent them out, at first together and later in pairs,
to spread His message themselves and do precisely as He Himself
was doing.

Jesus never hid Himself. He showed Himself ready to speak
to any who would some to see Him or speak with Him, be they
scribes, Pharisees, Sadducees, or doctors of the law; He gave fresh
interpretations of the Jewish Scriptures, expounded the facets of
His own message in vivid memorable stories and won many to a
new insight and firmer faith in the religion of their ancestors.

Peter's Recognition

At last, while at Caesarea Philippi, He asked His disciples
whom they thought Him to be, and Simon Peter answered, " Thou
art the Christ, the Son of the living God ", with sudden insight
conferred upon him by his " Father in heaven ", not by " flesh
and blood " [2].

Some three years had passed since His baptism and Jesus
turned towards Jerusalem making His way slowly, so as to be there
for the Feast of the Passover. He entered the city riding on a colt
or young donkey a week before the Passover and was received
by the people with cheering and excited anticipation. He at once
visited the Temple of Solomon, indignantly drove out money-changers who were using its precincts for trade, and publicly promulgated
His message.

Arrest, trial and death

The acclamations of the people, the crowds who listened
to Him, the authoritative and unanswerable replies to test questions
from the learned, the challenges to tradition and the vigorous
purging of the Temple decided the priestly hierarchy that Jesus
must be put away. One of His disciples, Judas Iscariot, had become
disillusioned over his hopes that Jesus would re-establish the

11

Kingdom of David, and was easily suborned. Judas led the priests' armed men to where Jesus was with His disciples, and they arrested Him. There was a scuffle but the arrest was successful; there was no attempt at rescue.

After private investigation before Caiaphas, the high priest, public accusation before Pontius Pilate followed. On interrogation, Jesus made His first and only public avowal of His station. Pontius Pilate, the Roman ruler of Judaea, handed Him over to the priests for verdict, himself unconvinced of His guilt but afraid of the consequences if a religious problem was not handled to the satisfaction of the local divines. Jesus was condemned to death, scourged, mocked and finally taken out to a hill on the outskirts of the city, where he was crucified with two bandits.

Recollections on the Cross

What must have been the thoughts of Jesus as He hung there in agony and humiliation before the gaze of a hostile crowd?

Memories of many kinds must surely have come to Him, of the polyglot inhabitants of Egypt where He spent His earliest days, of His quiet upbringing in Nazareth with His younger brothers and sisters, of His visits to the Temple and His early discussions with the learned He found there, of His exercise of the carpenter's craft for His family and His neighbours, of the early intimations of His mission which withheld Him from accepting the responsibility of marriage and children of His own, of His meeting with John the Baptist and His awakening to His full station of Messiahship, involving total subservience to the will of His Father, total abnegation of all personal interests and desires.

Perhaps too He recalled how the reactions of the learned divines and of His audiences in the synagogues quickly showed that the only means open for spreading His Gospel was through the poor, the illiterate, the under-privileged common folk among whom He had selected His disciples. No doubt He recollected how He had held large throngs of people spellbound with His words, how He had moved them to share with one another what they had with them until they discovered there was more than enough for all, " by twelve basket loads;" then there were the lepers, the blind, the ague-ridden, the crippled, the withered, the paralysed, even the " dead " whose health He had helped to renew through their faith in Him until their spiritual life was reinvigorated for all time.

Surely He remembered the way He had led His disciples through constant association, through example, through exhortation, through parable and explanation, through test and imitation of His ways, to a growing realisation of His true station and purpose, until the great moment of Simon Peter's joyful awestruck announcement such a short time before the end.

He must have lived again the last week of His life, His entry into Jerusalem amid the plaudits of the fickle crowd, the invariable verbal victories over the Scribes, Pharisees and Sadducees, His last meal with His disciples when in the upper room of heightened consciousness all had felt to the full His vibrant, never to be forgotten tenderness and His radiant love for them all, His walk in the Garden of Gethsemane, His last meditation near His sleeping disciples, His betrayal, Peter's triple denial of acquaintance with Him, His triumphant proclamation before Pilate and before Caiaphas and the assembled priesthood, and His final hours of torture and scorn.

Had He failed His Father? No, he had done all that could be done in the time. Small wonder that He cried out, as He foresaw the spreading radiance of His glorious spirit carried through the planet by His devoted followers destined to grow to multitudes, " Lord, how Thou has glorified me!" [3].

Jesus was fastened to the cross at the ninth hour in the morning. At about noon the sky was darkened. At three in the afternoon He cried out and died.

Joseph of Arimathea asked Pilate for the body, took it down, wrapped it and placed it in a rock tomb in the presence of several of Jesus' women followers, completing his task before the Sabbath commenced.

Realisation that Jesus still lived

On the day after the Sabbath, realisation dawned upon the inner eye of those who had been closest to Him that His reality was not dead but still very much alive. First Mary of Magdala, then Peter and the other disciples (except Judas who committed suicide), then others who had known Him, realised this truth, heard His words again ringing in their ears, and determined to spread His cause and His teachings to the ends of the earth in the assurance that He would always be with them. The vividness of those impressions was so intense that it was as if He still walked and talked with His followers. But the vividness lasted only a short while.

Day of Pentecost

Forty days after the crucifixion, on the day of Pentecost, the eleven remaining disciples and other believers were gathered to choose a replacement for Judas. After they had elected Matthias they consulted about their future. So earnestly and intently did they consult that their hearts were kindled with eager fiery zeal and each resolved to sacrifice his all to spread the cause of Jesus to the ends of the earth. Never in history had there been such radiant effective unanimity.

" The disciples of Christ forgot themselves and all earthly things, forsook all their cares and belongings, purged themselves of self and passion and with absolute detachment scattered far and wide and engaged in calling the peoples of the world to the Divine

13

Guidance, till at last they made the world another world, illumined the surface of the earth and even to their last hour proved self-sacrificing in the pathway of that Beloved One of God. Finally in various lands they suffered glorious martyrdom."[4]

Proof of Divinity

Stripped of all the supernatural embellishment, the legendary stories of His conception, birth, death and the elements of the miraculous, concerning which believers and sceptics have wrangled through the centuries whether true or untrue, the story still remains remarkable. That One Man, after only two or three years of active ministry in an obscure corner of the Roman Empire, culminating, only a week or two before He was put to a bandit's death, in the acknowledgement of His true reality by only one other man, should have so imbued His followers with the effective truth of His cause that they were able to transform the planet, is more than adequate proof in itself of the divine origin of the Mission of Jesus. That entire nations and peoples full of inveterate prejudice and hatred for one another, like the lion and the lamb, should within a few generations become reconciled by the cause of Jesus is sufficient evidence that that cause was of God, for in those early years the followers of Jesus had no advantage of wealth, power, prestige to help them in their open challenge to the religious and social practice of the times. Yet how gloriously they triumphed!

" Know thou that when the Son of Man yielded up His breath to God, the whole creation wept with a great weeping. By sacrificing Himself, however, a fresh capacity was infused into all created things. Its evidences, as witnessed in all the peoples of the earth, are now manifest before thee. The deepest wisdom which the sages have uttered, the profoundest learning which any mind hath unfolded, the arts which the ablest hands have produced, the influence exerted by the most potent of rulers, are but manifestations of the quickening power released by His transcendant, His all-pervasive and resplendent Spirit" [5].

Chapter 2

INTERPRETATION OF SCRIPTURE

Jesus many times spoke of Himself as light: " I am the light of the world: he that followeth me shall not walk in darkness, but shall have the light of life" [1], " As long as I am in the world, I am the light of the world" [2], " I am come a light into the world, that whosoever believeth on me should not abide in darkness" [3] Clearly, this light of which He spoke was not literally light in the sense the light that shines from a torch, an electric bulb, or even the sun. It was not something that could be measured on a photometer as a cameraman measures light intensity when he wants to take a good photograph. If it is not the light of the physical world, what did Jesus mean?

In His wonderful reply to Nicodemus, Jesus said, " And no man hath ascended up to heaven, but he that came down from heaven, even the Son of man which is in heaven" [4]. As Jesus was there speaking and present in person to His disciples, yet He declared that He was at the same time in heaven. Although born of Mary, yet He said He came down from heaven. What is meant, then, by " heaven ", " coming down from heaven ", and " ascending up to heaven?"

Again, the Greek word " pneuma ", of which the English translation is " spirit ", means breath, just as " spirit ", deriving from the Latin word " spiritus ", also originally meant breath. Is it to be thought that the breath that we breathe is meant whenever the word " pneuma " or " spirit " is used? " Verily, verily, I say unto thee, Except a man be born of water and of the spirit, he cannot enter the kingdom of God. That which is born of the flesh is flesh; and that which is born of the spirit is spirit" [5]. " The spirit is willing, but the flesh is weak" [6].

Jesus came to a world out of touch with the world of God. the stars of guidance of the past had become darkened and obscured; Wealth, influence with authority, knowledge of tradition attracted honour among men, not the goodness of motive, of soul, of deeds. Apathy, abnormality, self-centredness, stony indifference prevailed. Jesus, in a special, unique compelling way, showed in every act, movement, word and manner, with undeviating steadfastness, a link to another realm of reality, a practical alternative to the prevailing condition of the world. His calm, memorable expression of love, of truth, of justice acted like a radiant light upon the souls of the receptive enabling them to realise a new mode of living, a new dimension of existence. Aspiration to better things is inherent in the soul of men. With the new door of hope opened before them men were charged with fresh energy, fresh vitality. Thus radiating the light of the spiritual Sun of Truth from the heaven of the religion of God, Jesus was able in many cases to heal the blindness of the inner eye of the soul and inspire to new activity for the furtherance of human progress. His ' light ' from ' heaven ' dispelled spiritual ' blindness ', gave a fresh direction to the birds of men's hearts with ampler degree of life or ' spirit '.

Jesus said He came to judge the world, " For judgement I am come into this world, that they which see not might see; and that they which see might be made blind " [7], and He added to the Pharisees, " If ye were blind, ye shall have no sin: but now ye say, ' We see '; therefore your sin remaineth " [8], and again, " If I had not come and spoken unto them, they had not had sin: but now they have no cloke for their sin " [9]. There is no record of Jesus making anyone blind who could see physically. The existence of sin is made dependent on the absence of blindness, indeed it is made to depend on the coming of Jesus. When Jesus spoke of the Pharisees, He said on another occasion, " Let them alone: they be blind leaders of the blind. And if the blind lead the blind, both shall fall into the ditch " [10].

The examples can be multiplied over and over again. " Light ", " heaven ", " spirit ", " blindness " all mean something other than their literal, physical meanings when Jesus used the words. The contexts compel us to interpret otherwise, " Blindness " clearly means lack of inner vision or insight; " spirit " means principle of vitality or animating principle; " heaven " means a special state or condition of consciousness or exalted realm of being; " light " means radiating life-giving truth, justice, beauty, love. All the words have abstract meanings, not concrete, physical meanings.

So often Jesus said, " Who hath ears to hear, let him hear " [11], " It is the spirit that quickeneth; the flesh profiteth nothing; the words that I speak unto you, they are spirit, and they are life " [12].

To take the sayings of Jesus literally " profiteth nothing ". How different, perhaps, would have been the history of the past 2000 years if instead of taking Jesus literally, the followers of Jesus had taken his every act, His every parable, His every circumstance, His every saying as if it had a primary spiritual meaning. There could then never have developed the incrustation of superstition or the conflict with reason and with science which has rendered the glorious faith of Christ a dead letter, non-effective in the minds and hearts of people today.

Those who make the effort, with prayerful heart and soul turned to Christ Himself, can even now cut right back to those eternal truths and meanings with which His every word was so potently charged that He could say, " Heaven and earth shall pass away, but my words shall not pass away " [13].

16

Those things that so cruelly divide the community of Christians need never have arisen. The meanings of the words of Jesus, if taken with inner vision, would never have caused dissension, because the ocean of such meanings could never be plumbed. Only when the words and actions are taken literally is it inevitable that differences arise since everyone thinks he understands and experiences those things in a way that can be crystallised into forms which everyone can accept. Hence the creeds, hence the sacraments, hence the rituals and ceremonies, hence the dogmas and all those fruitless theological hair-splittings which have been the ultimate cause of prejudice, hatred, rancour, war, partisanship, and eventually of disillusionment, materialism, hopelessness and misery for countless millions.

How true is it that an instrument, intended like a lamp to illumine the whole house and serve the needs of all, can become in the hands of a wilful child or a blind man the means of burning the house down!

17

Chapter 3

SOME PROBLEMS

" Before the cock crow twice, thou shalt deny me thrice "[1]
" The cock shall not crow till thou hast denied me thrice "[2]

It can scarcely be wrong to take his warning in a literal sense as a prevision of Peter's temporary lapse of confidence. The detail given is too specific. Yet the purpose of the inclusion of the story may well hold deeper spiritual significance than has hitherto been acknowledged. Despite his momentary diffidence, no doubt induced by the surroundings and by the apparent collapse of hopes set on the newly acknowledged Messiah, now held in custody, to restore the glory of Israel, Peter, as the record shows, went on to develop qualities of leadership and staunch loyalty culminating in his martyrdom or total self-sacrifice far from the Galilee of his birth. The incident may thus be taken as a mighty proof of the power of the spirit working through a vessel of demonstrated frailty.

A further explanation is tentatively offered. Jesus spoke of His sending a Comforter[3], of His own return[4], of the coming of the Spirit of Truth[5]—three events. The Christian community, embodied symbolically at the time by Peter alone, was to fail to recognise Him on any of the three occasions. He returned in the person of the Comforter when the Prophet Muhammad came; He Himself returned in the person of the Bab, Whose ministry constitutes an extraordinary parallel to that of Christ, matching it point by point in innumerable ways; He returned in the glory of the Father in the person of Baha'u'llah Whose Teachings comprise the Spirit of Truth in a world come of age. Proof of these assertions can be at once seen by the unbiassed in the fruits of their work and missions in relation to the evolution of human society.

Substance for this explanation of the words of Christ can be added from the threefold injunction He gave to Peter[6] to feed His sheep, with the corollary questions, " Simon, son of Jonas, lovest thou Me?" The implied warning that Peter, symbolising the Christian community, might lapse from such love and fail to feed His sheep with the unadulterated food of the spirit, seems clear enough. Why else the reiteration? After all, the Master of the house may come " at even, or at midnight, or at the cockcrowing, or in the morning "[7] and alertness is therefore enjoined, again three times[8].

18

There is yet another hint at this deeper, wider meaning in the account of the disciples in Gethsemane. Three times Jesus went apart to pray and three times He requested His three closest disciples and admonished them to keep watch, but three times He finds they have fallen asleep when He returns to them. " The spirit truly is ready, but the flesh is weak ":[9] the disciples, representing the Christian church and community, three times were to show themselves inadequately prepared, insufficiently vigilant, too wrapped in a strange slumber when He returned.

" In the beginning was the word, and the word was with God, and the word was God ".[10]

The sublime words at the opening of John's Gospel seem to have been taken from an antiphonal hymn. Wherever they are from, this passage provides a theological idea of great subtlety and depth of meaning. An approach to part of this meaning may be made by recollecting that individual letters do not of themselves constitute a complete concept, whereas a word comprising several letters has a complete significance and independent sense. So individual followers, such as disciples or other believers, cannot of themselves represent independent meanings as their significance is a dependent one, but Christ expressed the perfect meaning of divine reality and embodied a total significance as He was the Word of God.

But Christ was a pure reed, a perfect mirror and provided a channel for, or reflected perfectly, the divine attributes which were focused through Him. The rays of the Sun of Truth were not separated from their Source when reflected and focused, they were still with God, they were God, but the reed or the mirror did not have to become identical with the Source of Light to be a perfect instrument for that Source. The Sun of Truth did not have to descend to the realm of the mirror but remained in lofty inaccessible condition. The essential Reality of Christ, His Christhood, was the embodiment of the divine virtues and attributes of God.

The entire creation is present to its Creator from the beginning that has no beginning to the end that has no end, in all the wonder of its evolving capacity to reflect the irradiating qualities of the Creator; just as to the sun in the heavens there is no division of time. The entire process of the great cycle of existence is one meaning to its Creator, a significance which becomes explicit as it is caused to unfold through those perfect Intermediaries Whose will is wholly subordinate to the Will of God. Each such Intermediary, each Founder-Prophet of the great divine religions, expresses that meaning successively in greater measure as the maturing evolving capacity of creation evolves to receive it. Each therefore is essentially identical, one with another, though different in name, in immediate

19

mission, in geographical home. Thus Christ can say, " Before Abraham was, I am ",[11] " I go away and come again unto you ",[12] " If I go not away, the Comforter will not come unto you, but if I depart, I will send him unto you ",[13] " I have yet many things to say unto you, but ye cannot bear them now. Howbeit when he,* the Spirit of Truth, is come, he will guide you into all truth ",[14] " And other sheep I have, which are not of this fold ";[15] yet He can also say, " I am the way, the truth and the life; no man cometh unto the Father, but by me "[16] and " The Son of man shall come in the glory of his Father ".[17]

One of the many meanings of the oneness of father, son and spirit can thus be understood, and the mercy of God implied in the statement that the Father " maketh his sun to rise on the evil and the good, and sendeth rain on the just and unjust "[18] surely means that none has been deprived of the bestowals of God.

The proof of the Word of God and the validity of the Intermediary between the Creator and His creation consists in the penetration and potency of the Word, the teachings of that Intermediary in the cultivation of heavenly attributes in the hearts and lives of the followers and the bestowal of divine education upon the world of humanity. The emergence of great civilisations in history, based on religion, is itself a sufficient proof of the validity of each Founder Prophet of religion as an Intermediary with God, as an embodiment of the Christhood of Christ. " Ye shall know them by their fruits ".[19]

* It should be noted that in the original Greek it is clearly a person, " that man ", who possesses a tongue, for he is to speak, and an ear, for he is to hear. The words, " the Spirit of Truth ", are adjectival and descriptive of " that man ", not the other way round, as is clear from the grammar. Thus it is not sense to suppose, as some seem to do, that this prophecy was fulfilled at Pentecost.

Chapter 4

WHAT JESUS DID NOT TEACH

'This people draweth nigh unto me with their mouths, and honoureth me with their lips; but their heart is far from me. But in vain they do worship me, teaching for doctrines the commandments of men ".[1]

Before we attempt to outline the true teachings of Jesus, we should review some of the things which have been wrongly attributed to Him by different groups of His followers from time to time. There is such a long list of these things that only a selection of some of the more important can be made.

Asceticism

Jesus Himself was described by His enemies as " gluttonous and a wine-bibber ".[2] He was contrasting Himself with John the Baptist who was genuinely ascetic. Jesus did of course encourage His followers to fast,[3] but He also made it clear that provided they placed first their efforts for establishing His kingdom in the hearts, everything else would be added[4]: there is no indication of non-enjoyment or prohibition of the good things of life when they are available and do not distract from or claim prior attention over the main purpose.

John the Baptist was ascetic, but his mission was a special one of brief duration only. Asceticism could not be a divine injunction since its effects are to diminish the powers of the body. If perfection could be attained by ascetic disciplines bringing about control of the passions through prolonged training and abstinence, thus weakening desire, then the ideal would be a dead body which is totally bereft of desires and passions.

A man cannot be " defiled " by what goes into the mouth[5]

When Jesus enjoined His followers to become as little children,[6] He meant that adults must use their adult powers to choose to practise the innocence, sinlessness and guileless candour of children rather than their opposites, not that they should so weaken themselves as to become childlike through inability to be otherwise.

Celibacy

Some people have made much of the fact that Jesus never married, supposing that ideally a celibate state is preferable to marriage. Such a view is a travesty of good sense and contrary to

21

the spirit of the general Gospel teachings. Jesus never married because He was aware, from the beginning of the inevitable outcome of His mission, that He must sacrifice His life for the truth He proclaimed, and because He knew the kind of life He would have to lead during His ministry. He could never have asked a woman to share His life which He once described thus, " The foxes have holes, and the birds of the air have nests; but the Son of man hath not where to lay his head ".[7]

Once, when challenged by Sadducees regarding the relationship of a woman who married each of seven brothers in turn, taking them successively as each died without offspring, Jesus said, " The children of this world marry, and are given in marriage: but they which shall be accounted worthy to obtain that world, and the resurrection from the dead, neither marry nor are given in marriage ".[8] But here Jesus is answering a specific question about relationship between man and woman after death, and He went on, " Neither can they die any more ".

The whole setting of the Gospels and the spirit of their teachings pre-suppose the continuity of the law of Moses except when specifically modified, and the law of Moses has much to say about wives and marriage. Jesus clearly refers to the divine intention underlying creation, " Have ye not read, that he which made them at the beginning made them male and female ".[9]

Jesus' evident love for children also clearly pre-supposes that children shall continue to be born and be born in wedlock.

Children are the fruit of the tree of the union of a man and his wife; their upbringing is a challenge to the quality of their parents. But for that challenge a whole range of human attributes, latent in everyone, must remain without outlet and expression. To advocate celibacy is to deny the very fruit of the tree of the planet itself and logically to encourage the gradual termination of the human race, the purpose of the planet's creation; the true Christianity of Jesus is nowhere inconsistent with reason.

Original Sin

Strange views have been expressed by intelligent men on the subject of original sin. Interpreting literally the allegorical story of Adam and Eve, some people have supposed that in some way the fall of Adam, through succumbing to Eve's temptation to disobey God's strict command about an apple leading to his banishment from the Garden of Eden, was visited upon all later generations of mankind everywhere until, through an oblatory self-sacrifice on the cross, Jesus Christ redeemed those who turned to Him and believed on Him and thus atoned for the sin of Adam.

The ramifications of the developed doctrine have even led to the supposition that this remarkable form of salvation was due to the absence of a human father and the immaculacy, at conception

22

of Jesus, of Mary as Virgin Mother. Because of the extraordinary, indeed supernatural, miracle entailed, Jesus must have been God Himself incarnate and Mary, as Mother of God, must also have warranted mystical stature and bodily resurrection.

People who hold these views overlook so many things. Jesus said, "If I had not come and spoken unto them (the Jews, or the people of the world) they had not had sin, but now they have no cloke for their sin. He that hateth me hateth my Father also. If I had not done among them the works which none other man did, they had not had sin: but now have they both seen and hated both me and my Father ".[10] He also said, "And as touching the dead, that they rise, have ye not read in the Book of Moses, how in the bush God spoke unto Him, saying: I am the God of Abraham, and the God of Isaac, and the God of Jacob? He is not the God of the dead, but the God of the living: ye do therefore greatly err ".[11] "Had ye believed Moses, ye would have believed me ".[12]

We do not regard it as just to condemn a man for what his father did before him, still less for what a distant ancestor did. How, then, can we impute lesser standards of justice to God Himself?

The wonderful story of Adam and Eve is intended to be an allegory referring to man, the species, who has always been and will always be susceptible to temptation, for that is the way man is made. His personal ego, or natural proclivities, the serpent or satan, will always try to tempt his soul, Eve, which governs the actions of his body, Adam, to depart from the strict injunctions of God. This is and will continue for ever to be innate in all men. Only detachment from the world of nature through rebirth or conversion to the teachings of God, leading to self-mastery, can free a man to start becoming a true human, with the human virtues, at the same time putting away the vices which pertain to his animal self. "That which is born of the flesh is flesh; and that which is born of the spirit is spirit ".[13]

Incarnation

Many people have come to suppose that Jesus should be regarded as God Himself come down from heaven occupying human form until release after death on the cross. This strange view seems to have arisen from interpreting certain statements made by Jesus Himself, taken in isolation, or from the supposition that certain of the recorded miracles, considered literally, could only have been performed by the Godhead. The desire to establish Christianity as a unique religion, to be distinguished from all other religions, and to be joined by all peoples who, in order to join it, had to repudiate the foundation of their own natal religion, led to even greater emphasis on those things which might be shown to prove it to be unique, full, perfect, sufficient for all time. This emphasis has been made at the

23

expense of other passages in the Gospels which are either explained away as interpolations or inaccuracies, or merely ignored and passed over.

Jesus is therefore regarded as in Himself the complete fulfilment of all the Old Testament prophecies. The apparently supernatural elements of His conception, birth, baptism, teaching activities, acts of compassion, death, resurrection, ascension, are given every possible prominence at Sunday School, in sermons, in liturgies, in sacraments. The Pentecostal consultation of the disciples is marked as the consummation of Jesus' own prophecy to send the Spirit of Truth to lead men to all truth. The orthodox churches, as successors to the communities established by the disciples, have come to regard themselves as depositories of that Spirit of Truth organised to deliver it in measured quantities to meet the evolving requirements of their own membership. The accredited representatives of those churches, by means of ceremonial transference of grace through ordination, or ' laying on of hands ', in supposedly direct succession from the apostles themselves, are then regarded as mediating, in intensity proportionate to rank, contact with the originating source of apostolic appointment, namely Jesus, in other words God Himself. Those making such contact may then be moved to a sense of appropriate ecstasy through the point of mediation. This reaches its strongest sense where the belief is also accepted that the bread and wine of the mass or communion are transmuted in substance (essence), though not outwardly, into the actual person and blood of Jesus, in other words, of God Himself.

The possibilities of non-rational mysticism are then exploited to the full so as to strengthen and sustain the spiritual fetters of the faithful. The faithful, in pain of forfeiture of paradise itself, are then subjected to a wide range of other demands, for regularity of confession and church attendance, for ' voluntary ' contribution to ecclesiastical expense and overheads, for reluctantly and expensively granted dispensations from a wide range of ecclesiastically devised misdemeanours, for conformity to expensive rituals at times of birth, puberty, death, for sanctification of relics, images, representations, for acceptance of fresh dogma however contradictory to plain sense or to science, for recognition of cures, visions, voices as miraculous.

Influence has even been brought to bear on the opinions of the faithful in secular, political matters. Wars have been started up or strongly supported and other kinds of violence engendered against heretics, unbelievers, Jews and other non-conforming groups.

All these things seem to have stemmed from the following propositions or recorded statements:—

1. Peter's recognition of the station of Jesus, " Thou art the Christ, the Son of the living God ".[14]

2. The words of Jesus, " Thou art Peter, and upon this rock I will build my church; and the gates of hell shall not prevail against

it. And I will give unto thee the keys of the kingdom of heaven, and whatsoever thou shalt bind on earth shall be bound in heaven: and whatsoever thou shalt loose on earth shall be loosed in heaven ".[15]

3. "I am the way, the truth and the life: No man cometh unto the Father, but by me. If ye had known me, ye should have known my Father also: and from henceforth ye know him, and have seen him ".[16]

4. "He that hath seen me hath seen the Father . . . believe me that I am in the Father, and the Father in me ".[17]

5. "Ye have not chosen me, but I have chosen you, and ordained you, that ye should go and bring forth fruit, and that your fruit should remain ".[18]

6. "And the Lord said unto the servant, "Go out into the highways and hedges, and compel them to come in, that my house may be filled ".[19]

7. "All power is given unto me in heaven and in earth. Go ye therefore, and teach all nations, baptizing them in the name of the Father, and of the Son, and of the Holy Ghost; teaching them to observe all things whatsoever I have commanded you: and, lo, I am with you always, even unto the end of the world ".[20]

8. "Heaven and earth shall pass away: but my words shall not pass away ".[21]

9. "As thou has sent me into the world, even so have I also sent them into the world. And for their sakes I sanctify myself, that they also might be sanctified through the truth. Neither pray I for these alone, but for them also which shall believe on me through their word; that they all may be one; as thou, Father, art in me, and I in thee, that they also may be one in us; that the world may believe that thou hast sent me. And the glory which thou gavest me I have given them; that they may be one, even as we are one: in them, and thou in me, that they may be made perfect in one; and that the world may know that thou hast sent me, and hast loved them, as thou hast loved me. Father, I will that they also, whom thou hast given me, be with me where I am; that they may behold my glory, which thou hast given me: for thou lovedst me before the foundation of the world ".[22]

10. "Take, eat; this is my body ".[23]

11. "Drink ye all of it; for this is my blood of the New Testament which is shed for many for the remission of sins ".[24]

12. "With men this is impossible: but with God all things are possible ".[25]

A number of other passages may be quoted in support of the authority claimed by those who hold the views set out above, but these are a reasonably representative selection.

Some of the views and interpretations are discussed in other sections of this chapter. Here we confine ourselves to the question of incarnation which in itself was the subject of prolonged theological dispute over an iota. Was Jesus to be regarded as of ' one substance with the Father ', or ' of like substance with ' the Father? The difference lay in the spelling of a certain Greek adjective which meant one or the other depending on the presence or absence of the letter ' i ', iota.

Fortunately, Jesus said many things about the relationship with God, not just those things that have been quoted. The problem is to reconcile in a logical way the different things He did say, some of which suggest identity with, some difference from, God.

Jesus as Messiah

" What think ye of Christ? Whose son is he?", asked Jesus of the Pharisees and when they said, " The son of David ", Jesus said, " How then doth David in spirit call him Lord, saying, ' The Lord said unto my Lord, sit thou on my right hand, till I make thine enemies thy footstool?'.[26] " If David then call him Lord, how is he his son?"[27]

This passage establishes the claim of Jesus, the Christ, to be the spiritual Messiah of the Jews in a way not challenged or answered by the Pharisees. It is reinforced both by Peter's recognition of Jesus as " the Christ, the Son of the living God "[28] and by Jesus' own acknowledgement both then and during the interrogation before Caiaphas, the high priest and the assembled scribes and elders when Caiaphas said, "I adjure thee by the living God, that thou tell us whether thou be the Christ, the Son of God ", and Jesus answered, "Thou hast said "[29] and again later, when Pontius Pilate asked, " Art thou the King of the Jews?" and Jesus replied, " Thou sayest ".[30]

Jesus then is established as:

i the Christ (from a Greek word meaning 'anointed ');

ii the son of God.

iii the son, or descendant, of David (at least in the view of the Pharisees);

iv the Messiah of the Jews;

v David's Lord in the spirit.

Divine and physical birth

Yet Jesus' descent from David depends on Joseph, his mother Mary's husband. Many passsages indicate that Jesus was the physical offspring of David's line through Joseph.[31]

Jesus then was chosen of God to be born of Mary, a fact that was intimated to her in the spirit. Mary was an unmarried virgin (or young woman) when she conceived. If Jesus was the Messiah of the Jews, He was of the seed of David and Joseph was His physical father. If Joseph was not the physical father, then Jesus was not of the seed of David and was not wholly the fulfilment of the Jewish expectation. If Jesus was not wholly the Messiah, then another was to come after Him. This of course does not mean that the Jews should not have acknowledged Him as the light of the world, the Sun of Truth for His age. It would mean that they were also right to look for another Messiah in a later age.

It is perhaps at this point worth reminding ourselves that the coincidence of physical and spiritual conception occurs also in the story of the birth of Isaac when Abraham was one hundred years old and Sarah ninety years old.[32]

" And the Lord visited Sarah as he had said, and the Lord did unto Sarah as he had spoken. For Sarah conceived and bore Abraham a son in his old age, at the set time of which God had spoken to him ".[33]

Similarly, the birth of John the Baptist had both a spiritual and a physical coincidence.[34]

We may therefore surely conclude:

1.   Jesus was conceived and born physically of a pure un-married young woman, the Virgin Mary, thereby fulfilling the prophecy of Isaiah, " Therefore the Lord himself shall give you a sign: behold, a virgin (young woman) shall conceive, and bear a son, and shall call his name Immanuel ".[35]

2.   Jesus was begotten or conceived spiritually of the Holy Spirit of God.[36]

3.   Either Jesus was begotten physically by Joseph, or if not so begotten He could not have been of David's line (see above). There still remains a mystery, but is this really important?

◁ The greatness of Jesus Christ consists in His perfections which derived from God, not from the fact of a virgin birth. If His greatness depended on having no physical father then the Jewish expectations remained incompletely fulfilled and we should revere Adam even more than Jesus since Adam was born without either father or mother.

Jesus distinct fom God (i.e. not God made man)

In many places Jesus made it very clear that He and God were distinct from each other. He said, " Why callest thou me good? There is none good but one, that is God "[37] and again, " But of that day and that hour knoweth no man, no, not the angels which are in heaven, neither the son, but the Father ".[38]

The parable of the vineyard and the wicked husbandmen also clearly distinguishes between the son who is slain and the lord of the vineyard who will come and destroy the husbandmen.[39]

Jesus also said, " My Father is greater than I ",[40] and " And I will pray the Father ",[41] and " I go to the Father ",[42] and again, " When ye have lifted up the Son of man, then shall ye know that I am he, and that I do nothing of myself, but as my Father hath taught me, I speak these things ".[43]

How could Jesus more emphatically repudiate identity with God than by stating that God alone was good, that God was greater than he, that he merely spoke as God taught Him, that God possessed knowledge which was withheld from Him?

Jesus as a prophet (i.e. a forth-teller, a preacher, a predictor of events)

Jesus was referring to Himself when He said, " Verily, I say unto you, No prophet is accepted in his own country ",[44] and again, " A prophet is not without honour, but in his own country and among his own kin, and in his own house ".[45]

Jesus as a messenger of God (i.e. one sent)

Numerous passages in the Gospels indicate that Jesus regarded himself as sent into the world by God the Father.[46]

He said, for instance, " I must preach the kingdom of God to other cities also; for therefore am I sent "[47]; and also, " My meat is to do the will of him that sent me, and to finish his work ".[48]

Conclusion

Jesus often called Himself the Son of man, acknowledged recognition three times as the Son of God, was regarded by contemporaries as the eldest son of the union of Mary and Joseph, referred to Himself as a prophet and a messenger of God, distinguished Himself carefully from identity with God, yet on several occasions indicated that He and the Father were one.

How can we reconcile these apparently conflicting statements?

If we compare God, the Father, the Essence of the Godhead, with the physical sun in the sky, then the sun's rays are the Holy Spirit, and the perfectly polished mirror turned to the sun is Jesus. The mirror reflects and focuses the full image of the sun. It is self-evidently not the sun itself, yet, if we look in it, we can see the sun wholly reflected in all its splendour. There is then a true logical trinity, the sun, the rays, and the light of the sun, the perfect reflection. In a sense they are one and the same, yet they obviously differ. The sun never descends from its place in the heavens to occupy the mirror, but he that looks at the mirror sees the sun.

Jesus possessed two natures. His human nature, with a physical body and a distinctive human personality, was similar in every way to that of other men, and like that of other men unique, unduplicated. Because of the body's limitations people found it difficult to recognise His inner reality; like the clouds over the sun, His body concealed His inner self. At the time of the last supper in the upper room,

28

He was standing before His disciples whole and healthy, when He invited them to eat the bread of His body and drink the wine of His blood; He was not transformed into bread and wine on that occasion. Unlike all others of His age, He was also born of the substance of God Himself, embodied His attributes, expounded His message, revealed His sovereignty, reflected the perfection of His beauty, transmitted His grace, mediated His knowledge and wisdom. In this sense He was identical with every other great prophet and messenger of God, Who founded a mighty revealed religion.

In relation to God, Jesus was a prophet, a messenger, a beloved Son, yet utterly self-effacing, totally subservient to God's will, all individuality wholly subordinated to the functions of mediating God to man as best it could be done at that time. In relation to man Jesus was at one with God since through Him and Him alone at that time were revealed to man the attributes and perfections and teachings of God, the will of God for man, in their entirety so far as man could bear them then.

The futility of the views of incarnation can be at once and most easily seen from the following propositions:—

God is Self-Subsistent, Unconditioned, Source of all Sources, Orb of the universe, Inaccessible, Unconstrained, Object of the adoration of the entire creation, Exalted above all attributes.

Man is finite, offspring of dust, inhabitant of one planet in one solar system of the boundless universe, susceptible to exigencies of nature such as need for food, drink, sleep, clothing, etc.

Were such a God to become incarnate in the concrete, limited form of a man He would thereby immediately cease to be God.

Baptism of Infants

Baptism is a symbolic action whereby the application of water, that unique substance so necessary for the physical life of all creatures which has also always been used for washing away dirt, represents outwardly an inward process whereby a human soul has commenced a cleansing of his inmost being through repentance and turning to the new source of life, putting away his old habits, ways and proclivities.

Baptism is thus a recognition, as end-result, of conversion or " second birth ": first natural birth, then later an awakening to the life of the spirit. To have meaning, such an awakening must clearly be conscious and responsible. As such it can pertain properly only to a mature adult fully aware of the meaning of his or her reaction, capable of self-control and competent to understand the consequences, duties and responsibilities of the new life of the spirit opening up ahead.

It was surely in this sense that Jesus accepted to be baptised Himself by John the Baptist, and it is surely in this sense that its practice should have been perpetuated by the disciples and later followers of Jesus.

29

John spoke of three ingredients to baptism; water, fire and spirit (or Holy Ghost): " I indeed baptise you with water unto repentence: but he that cometh after me (Jesus) is mightier than I, whose shoes I am not worthy to bear: he shall baptise you with the Holy Ghost and with fire ".[49]

Baptism with fire is meaningless if taken literally. It follows therefore that the inner meaning of all three ingredients must be sought.

Water may then be understood to symbolise knowledge and life, fire may be taken to mean the love of God, and the spirit the bounty of God. First knowledge, then response and enkindlement, and then the bountiful help of the power of the Holy Spirit to overcome and sustain. It is first to know, then to love and then to grow in faith. The bounty of God, the Holy Spirit, maintains the fire of God's love and assists to overcome past habits and future temptations.

How can any of this have meaning for an infant newly coined in the mint of life, without past habits and carnal proclivities, knowing nothing of the things of the spirit and totally unaware of the requirements and responsibilities of a spiritual life, capable if at all of only the most rudimentary degree of self-control?

Satan or the devil

Many have been so firmly imbued with the idea that Satan, or Lucifer, or the devil, exists as an entity distinct and real, that to state the opposite view is to cause bewilderment, outright rejection or even fearful supposition that one is an agent of Satan seeking a new way to tempt the true believer.

Yet it is the clear, simple, logical thing that must prevail, however deeply entrenched be the superstition and even if that superstition be based upon apparent scriptural authority.

Man is a creature with two natures, the physical nature which he shares with the animal, and the spiritual nature, or nature of non-physical degree, which comprises powers latent within him at birth, powers that grow and develop in response to directed effort. These abstract, intangible, non-physical powers or potentialities, grow and develop according to the direction of the effort made. That effort may be solely directed towards the satisfaction of man's physical needs and interests, towards attainment measured in terms of intellectual ability, position or success in this physical life. The effort may in addition and primarily be directed towards practising a life and following the precepts of God as mediated or interpreted by God's prophet, messenger and manifestation. The powers and potentialities evoked are very different in the two cases. In the one case, the reflection in the mirror of the heart turned towards the requirements of this physical life is dark and transient, as this physical life itself is transient and like a dark prison cell or womb. In the other case, the powers or potentialities can become illumined spiritual perfections adorning the soul or inmost reality.

This is the realm of free choice. In this sense alone does man possess free will.

The attachment to this physical life and its satisfactions is symbolised by the individual satan or devil which each one of us possesses and which accordingly constantly tempts us according to our own personal proclivities and interests. In a general way, universal because applicable to everyone, the scriptures sometimes refer to that which tempts, the evil whisperer in men's breasts, as Satan or the devil, as if it were in some way independent and distinct.

Jesus said, " There is nothing from without a man, that entering into him can defile him: but the things which come out of him, those are they that defile the man, If any man have ears to hear, let him hear ".[50] He also said, " Do not ye yet understand, that whatsoever entereth in at his mouth goeth into the belly, and is cast out into the draught? But those things which proceed out of the mouth come forth from the heart and they defile the man. For out of the heart proceed evil thoughts, murders, adulteries, fornications, thefts, false witness, blasphemies: these are the things which defile a man: but to eat with unwashen hands defileth not a man ".[51]

Again, " Either make the tree good, and his fruit good: or else make the tree corrupt and the fruit corrupt, for the tree is known by his fruit . . . A good man out of the good treasure of the heart bringeth forth good things: an evil man out of the evil treasure bringeth forth evil things ".[52]

Yet again, " Lay not up for yourselves treasures upon earth, where moth and rust doth corrupt, and where thieves break in and steal, but lay up for yourselves treasures in heaven where neither moth nor rust doth corrupt, and where thieves do not break in and steal: for where your treasure is, there will your heart be also ".[53]

How true it is that " every good thing is of God and every evil thing is of our own selves ".

Life is according to degree. The life of the mineral is less than that of the plant which contains it; the life of the plant is less than that of the animal which contains it; the life of the animal is less than that of the human which contains it. In relation to each higher degree the lower degree is, by comparison, like death or the relative absence of life. Also the lower degree is unable to comprehend the life of the higher degree, though lack of comprehension is no proof that such life does not exist still less that it is not a fuller life.

The life of the natural human is less than that of the human who is imbued with the spirit of faith, the bounty of the spirit engendered by the knowledge and love of God. Non-comprehension by the natural human of the life of the human imbued with the

31

spirit of faith is no proof that such a life does not exist still less that it is not a fuller life.

The life of the human imbued with the spirit of faith is capable of endless development as the spirit of faith is born of the knowledge and love of God and they are infinite. The life of the natural human is finite.

Although in relation to a higher degree of life the lower degree is as death or lifelessness, yet in its own degree it has life. It is futile to suppose otherwise. All creation is as if without life or existence when viewed from the standpoint of the reality of the divine Creator: a painting or a piece of sculpture is without life by comparison with the painter or sculptor himself, yet both in their own degree have existence and meaning.

No doubt it was to this that Jesus referred when he said, " Let the dead bury their dead "[54] indicating that those who were physically alive but spiritually dead could bury the physically dead, but the disciple in question should follow him, and live the higher fuller life of the spirit of faith.

Jesus said, " I am come that they might have life, and that they might have it more abundantly ".[55]

He also said, " Except a corn of wheat fall into the ground and die, it abideth alone: but if it die, it bringeth forth much fruit. He that loveth his life shall lose it: and he that hateth his life in this world shall keep it until life eternal. If any man serve me, let him follow me; and where I am, there shall also my servant be: if any man serve me, him will my Father honour ".[56]

Again, " Search the scriptures: for in them ye think ye have eternal life: and they are they which testify of me. And ye will not come to me, that ye might have life ".[57]

And again, " This is life eternal, that they might know thee the only true God, and Jesus Christ whom thou hast sent ".[58]

It is the undermining power of our own satanic selfish attachments and interests that saps the life we might otherwise have if we but will to know and love God and His messenger Jesus Christ, and make constant efforts to spend our lives and our resources in efforts to be like Him.

We are made potentially in the image and likeness of God, we are capable of mirroring the spiritual beauty and perfections of God. The capacity is engraved on our souls. Our choice is to seek God's help, through the spirit of faith in Jesus Christ, to make that capacity actual and growing, and thereby to enter into more abundant life. To do so, however, we need to make efforts to master our own selves, conquer our egoistic interests, control and put behind us our individual satan, submission to which can only deprive us of our birthright, the abundant rich life of the spirit, and through deprivation condemn us to our own individual private hell.

Non-violence

Some people have taken the words of Jesus, " And unto him that smiteth thee on the one cheek offer also the other ",[59] to mean that Jesus advocated the use of non-violent, passive response in all circumstances.

This clearly is wrong. If a malefactor is pardoned and left free to pursue his depredations without hindrance human affairs would quickly fall into total disorder and the foundations of human life would crumble.

Jesus was referring to the response of a person to another person, one to one, and was teaching avoidance of taking personal revenge. The same meaning should be attached to His words, " But I say unto you, that ye resist not evil: but whosoever shall smite thee on the right cheek, turn to him the other also ".[60] For a person struck by another person to strike back is but aggravating the situation. The second action is as reprehensible as the first, which itself, though wrong, arose in some way out of the inter-personal situation which existed only because there were two people in association with one another who had a kind of relationship (real or fancied) between them. If the first blow is felt to be necessary for satisfaction of a grievance then the opportunity for an unopposed second blow shows a desire to be sure of eliminating the cause of the grievance, and if the attitude be genuinely humble, to precipitate a change of heart.

The community however has the right to defend and protect itself for the general well-being. If a third party is present during a violent altercation between two people resulting in one striking the other, and the third party does not interfere he is being unjust towards the person struck. The third party must seek to prevent the blow. The order of community life depends on justice, not forgiveness; on adjustment of rights and acknowledgement of merits and deserts, not on overlooking offences.

Use of Force

There are several passages in the Gospels which seem to warrant the use of violence in certain circumstances:

1. Think not that I am come to send peace on earth: I came not to send peace, but a sword ".[61]

2. The cleansing of the Temple,[62] when Jesus overthrew the money-changers' tables and cast out the hucksters, the sheep, oxen and the doves, suggests violent action which is confirmed in John 2: 15 where reference is made to the use of " a scourge of small cords."

3. " And the lord said unto the servant, ' Go out into the highways and hedges, and compel them to come in, that my house may be filled ".[63]

33   C

The first of these passages can perhaps be thought of in more than one way. It can be taken in conjunction with the passage[64] in which Jesus foretells the effect of the spirit speaking, inspiring the words of his disciples, " And the brother shall deliver up the brother to death, and the father the child: and the children shall rise up against their parents, and cause them to be put to death. And ye shall be hated of all men for my name's sake . . ." The challenge to vested interests, established customs and conventional patterns of worship will cause violent reaction even within the family circle. The passage also, incidentally, clearly disavows any expectation that Jesus Christ came to establish the kingdom of God on earth as it is in heaven, that supreme event which is described in many a parable and prophesied in the sublime prayer all true believers are to use whenever they pray.

The cleansing of the Temple may describe an actual action of Jesus in which He gave full rein to the expression of indignation and was so vehement, and perhaps even supported by sympathisers, that the traffickers gave way and evacuated the holy precincts. The inner meaning of the action, regarded symbolically, can hardly be doubted: the worship of God and Mammon cannot coexist at the heart of the religion of God or in the human heart (the Temple); and the effect of the coming of Jesus was to drive out, at least temporarily, Mammon (the money-changers and hucketsers, etc.).

As to the compulsion of wayfarers to attend the special supper, which was used, it is said, to justify the execrable activities of the Spanish Inquisition, it should be noted that it forms part of a parable referring to the coming of the kingdom of God on earth when those who were invited, who knew about it and were nominal friends and persons of standing and substance, put selfish material interests first and refused the invitation, while the underprivileged and ignorant, wherever they might be, were to be constrained to replace them. Whenever a prophet of God appears the divines and the wealthy, who assume they know it all, fail to respond to His call, but the humbler people everywhere feel moved in spite of themselves, compelled by the power of spiritual attraction, unhindered by the thin eyelid of selfish greed.

Surely the clear imperative to Peter at the time of Jesus' arrest is the true teaching of Christianity about the use of force, " Put up again thy sword into his place: for all they that take the sword shall perish with the sword ".[65] If proof were needed of the departure of institutional Christianity from the true spirit of Christian teaching, there can be no clearer evidence than this that violent persecution of heretics (i.e. people with non-orthodox opinions) has taken place from very early times, 4th century A.D. onwards and a corrupt tree cannot bring forth any but evil and corrupt fruit.[66] No man can estimate the extent of the evil fruit which that corrupted tree has brought forth through the long centuries.

One of the strange consequences of division into sects and the crystallisation of divine religion into creeds and dogmas is the substitution of intellectual figments devised by learned thinkers for wider and simpler expositions, and deliberate overlooking or explaining away of clear statements of the Founder himself. This is the way superstition arises. Self-delusion and defensive reaction combine to elaborate the spiritual fetters which the authorities seek to impose on the faithful.

An example of this is the growth of worship paid to the Mother of Jesus, to the extent that she has even been supposed by some to have been taken up physically into the empyrean, in the same sort of way as Jesus himself, at death, From equality of destiny the step is short to equality of worshipful regard. Much of this seems to have sprung from the supposition that in order to have been free of original sin, itself a fanciful ecclesiastical fiction, Jesus must have been born from one who was herself in some miraculous way different from other humans, sinless, immaculate, unique and therefore possessed of a similar physical substance to that of Jesus. Logically one would suppose that such a view would entail equivalent treatment for Mary's own parents and their parents back to Adam and Eve, but such a conclusion is seemingly not drawn.

How clearly this attitude towards the Virgin Mary is at variance with historical fact as can be seen at once from the following:—

1. Jesus had brothers and sisters presumably born after him to his Mother Mary and Joseph.[67]

2. Except once, at the marriage of Cana when " his hour had not come ",[68] Mary is not recorded as playing any special part in the ministry of Jesus subsequent to His baptism by John the Baptist. It was Mary of Magdala who played the supremely important role of challenging Peter and the others to recognise that the Reality of Christ was not dead after the crucifixion. The stone of despair was rolled away from her inner eye and she saw Jesus as vitally vividly alive. So renewed was she in faith that she was able to arouse Peter and the disciples to similar insight and recognition.

3. Jesus was at pains to tell His followers that no special distinction on that account was to be paid to His mother and other members of His family just because of physical relationship.[69]

4. Just before His passing, on the cross, Jesus was at pains to ensure that His mother was cared for by " the disciple whom he loved "[70] who took her into his own home.

It is no derogation from His wonderful Mother, who had clearly recognised the uniqueness of Jesus from the early days of his mission, to say that Mary of Magdala was yet greater than she in the history of Christendom. It is surely a great disservice to her to try to make her out to be of other than human substance and so give her a falsely superstitious reverence, depriving her of her true

35

station as a supremely human person. She had been liable to be " a public example "[71] for being with child though she knew not a man; she had understood no more than her husband when Jesus as a child had said He had to be about His Father's business[72]; she had divined a special capacity in her Son for transmuting ordinary thirst-quenching water of merely verbal knowledge and relationship into the exhilarating wine of renewed faith[73]; on her bereavement at His death she had needed human consolation.

Miracles

How often did Jesus make it clear that He was not to be judged as a miracle-worker! Yet so many people centre their faith in Him on the miraculous, chiefly the miraculous physical resurrection, but also the other physical marvels ascribed to Him and taken by themselves at literal face value.

The story of the temptations in the wilderness was presumably related by Jesus Himself to His disciples from whom it came to be recorded. Otherwise this story, like the story of the ordeal in Gethsemane, would not be on record at all as no other person was present. To have related it Jesus must have meant to convey a special message, viz. the rejection of the miraculous, the spectacular and the use of force as methods for attracting souls. Yet each of these has been and continues to be used!

√ *Priestly Domination*

Those whom Jesus called to be His disciples were for the most part ordinary people, fisher folk. One or two may have been comparatively well educated, notably Judas Iscariot and Matthew Levi. None of them was a priest. Peter, given authority, because of the true quality of his faith, to bind and to loose, was not a priest, nor did his authority extend beyond himself or to adding to what Jesus had taught.

Nowhere in the Gospels is there warrant for the type of development which occurred whereby the control of the Christian religion came into the hands of the priests to shape as they thought fit. Indeed there are so many warnings about the subject that Jesus must have foreseen this development and the disastrous consequences that have since flowed from it.

To take but a few of these is to make the position crystal clear:

1. " Salt is good: but if the salt have lost his saltness, wherewith will ye season it? Have salt in yourselves, and have peace one with another ".[74]

In at least three ways the salt of the first disciples lost its savour

i Divisions occurred between the parts of the Church

ii The Word of God became adulterated with the commandments of men.

36

iii ⟨Ordinary people became deprived of the responsibility given them by Jesus to teach and preach the Word of God,⟩

⟵ These things are the result chiefly of self-arrogation of authority to interpret and to control. ⟩

2. " The disciple is not above his master, nor the servant above his lord ".[75]

Jesus left all that was needful for the successful prosecution of His faith and teachings. To add to that was to claim to know better, to be above the master (see also repeated warnings Jn. 13:16, 15:20).

3. " Ye know that they which are accounted to rule over the Gentiles exercise lordship over them; and their great ones exercise authority upon them. But so shall it not be among you: but whosoever will be great among you, shall be your minister: and whosoever of you will be the chiefest, shall be servant of all. For even the Son of Man came not to be ministered unto, but to minister, and to give his life a ransom for many ".[76]

Jesus performed none of the sacraments Himself except the eucharist and that in a manner vastly different from the way in which it has come to be performed. He enjoined baptism which was to be by water, by fire and by spirit. Where then are the special priestly functions? Services indeed He rendered, and He taught and preached, and He sacrified Himself.

4. " Beware of the leaven of the Pharisees which is hypocrisy ".[77]

" Take heed and beware of the leaven of the Pharisees and of the Sadducees ".[78]

" Take heed, beware of the leaven of the Pharisees, and of the leaven of Herod ".[79]

This Jesus warned His followers, knowing the danger they would be in of compromising His glorious principles and teachings.

The Concise Oxford Dictionary gives these definitions for Pharisee and Sadducee:

Pharisee: ' One of ancient Jewish sect distinguished by strict observance of traditional and written law and pretensions to sanctity '. Pharisees were patriotic, bigoted, ambitious, arrogant, and proudly self-righteous formalists.

Sadducee: ' A member of a Jewish sect or party that denied resurrection of the dead, existence of spirits and obligation of the traditional law '. Sadducees were identified with the wealthier hierarchy of the land and regarded only the written law as obligatory; they represented the opposite extreme from the Pharisees.

A Herodian was a member of a political party who supported the claim to sovereignty of the dynasty of Herod. There seem to have been two Herods at about that time: (1) Herod, son of Antipater, governor of Galilee from 47 B.C. and later King of Judea who died in 4 B.C. and was succeeded by his son Archelaus. (2) Herod Antipas, tetrarch of Galilee. The former decreed the death of the first born sons in Bethlehem at the time of Jesus' own birth. The latter had John the Baptist arrested and assented to his execution.

The meaning of these warnings of Jesus is now clear. His followers were to be vigilant lest their faith and their movement be infiltrated and eventually absorbed under the control of (*a*) bigoted formalists concerned with minute observance of tradition, (*b*) wealthier partisans of strict observance of the written code, (*c*) politically ambitious and worldly people. Bigotry, partisanship, fanaticism, reliance on tradition, personal ambition, worldliness— these were the dangers.

‹ 5. " Call no man your father upon the earth: for one is your Father, which is in heaven ".[80] ›

The context suggests that this does not relate to physical parenthood, for the followers are also enjoined not to allow themselves to be called " Rabbi " or " master ". The context implies that titles of any kind should be eschewed in the community of believing followers, for a rabbi was a Jewish doctor authorised by ordination to deal with law and ritual and to perform certain ceremonies.

‹ It would seem clear that Jesus expressly forbade people to be called ' Father ', or ' Padre ', or ' Doctor ' (religious), or ' Master ' (religious), and that He discouraged the use of any hierarchical titles at all. ›

6. The Parable of the Vineyard[81] clearly indicates that those in charge of religious affairs, the " husbandmen " of the Lord's vineyard, would be displaced when the Lord of the vineyard Himself came. This could only be right if they had departed from the pivotal teachings of the Lord given them through His Messengers and His Son. Is it not apparent that they have done just that, " teaching for doctrine the commandments of men "?[82]

Nevertheless it may be argued that sheep need a shepherd, that some form or organisation would be necessary after the spread of the faith occurred to a sufficient degree. This is true, but the safeguards were also expressed clearly enough. They must be shepherds, not hirelings, must love one another to the point of sacrifice of life for one another, must love their enemies, must look to the heart rather than to formal observance, must avoid titular elevation, vain repetitions, long extempore prayers, special types of vestment, particular privilege at social and religious gatherings, participation in partisan activity whether religious or secular, and at all times seek to live up to the standards of goodly behaviour and character established by the great Founder of their faith. Then indeed would they be " as eyes to the nations and true guides to men ".

The Sacraments

The meaning of a sacrament according to the Concise Oxford Dictionary, is ' Religious ceremony or act regarded as outward and visible sign of inward and spiritual grace (applied by the Eastern, Pre-Reformation Western, and Roman Catholic churches to the seven rites of baptism, confirmation, the eucharist, penance, extreme unction, orders and matrimony. restricted by most Protestants to baptism and the eucharist; the Sacrament, the Sacrament of the altar, the Blessed or Holy Sacrament, the eucharist, also the consecrated elements especially the bread or Host . . .)'.

So important are the sacraments, in whichever sense used, to much of present day Christianity that it has been said that Christianity is a ' sacramental religion '.

Here, perhaps, more than anywhere else, lies the point at which there has been a departure from the Christianity of Jesus, since only three of the seven recognised rites have any reference point at all in the Gospels, viz. those of baptism, of matrimony and of the eucharist The others—confirmation, penance, extreme unction, orders— have no such origin and are purely man-made accretions.

The inference from the definition is that in some way the inward and spiritual grace accompanies the outward and visible sign without which the grace would not reach, or descend to, the participants. For this there is no warrant at all.

The trouble seems to lie in a total misapprehension of the meaning of religion. Religion is not " reverence, awe, dependence, adoration and penitence ", to quote a recent pamphlet by Dr. Ramsey, Archbishop of Canterbury, though it may evoke or include those attitudes, feelings, realisations.

Objectively, i.e. as it were from the point of view of the Creator, " religion is the essential or necessary connection which proceeds from the reality of things ". In this sense religion is the Word or Holy Spirit delivered or mediated through the Founder of a divine faith, connected as He must be with the reality of things, with God. Subjectively, from man's point of view, " religion is an attitude to God expressed through life ", that is through our attitude to our fellow humans.

The purpose of a plant, a tree, an animal is the appearance of its flowers, fruits and best specific qualities. The purpose of man's creation is clearly the attainment of the highest human attributes, those which, being intangible, non-physical, accompany him, as part of his treasure in heaven, after departure from this mortal plane of existence. These attributes are potential, latent in each person's soul, and are developed through activity based on decisions or the exercise of will. We are heroes if we display courage in action where the action turns on personal choice between alternatives and knowledge of the consequences of the alternatives. We are not heroes because we know the meaning of the word courage however many the instances of courageous action that are familiar to us.

As man has two aspects, two directions to his reality, the physical and the spiritual, and as man can never free himself entirely from

39

the physical aspect or direction while he is still sentient, he needs counsel and guidance to help him choose the spiritual direction and recognise it for the better. Such counsel and such guidance stem from the Founders of the great religions who in turn are linked with the directing will of the Creator seeking to make man in His image to show forth to the utmost of his capacity His spiritual attributes. These spiritual attributes are " faith, certitude, justice, piety, righteousness, trustworthiness, love of God, inward peace, purity, detachment, humility, meekness, constancy, mercifulness, equity, compassion ". Everything must have a cause, a source, an origin. These attributes, though latent within every man, can only be brought into realisation by willed activity, the soul making of the will a door through which their steady growth is made possible, the soul turning to the Creator as known through His Messenger and drawing its sustenance and spiritual nurture from Him.

It follows therefore that the spiritual grace precedes the action and depends upon an active decision of man to turn for counsel and guidance towards the Founder of his religion, towards God. The external factor is purely incidental.

Thus the famous recognition of the station of Jesus by Peter was not shown him by flesh and blood but by his Father in heaven. He had turned his heart to the Father who had then endowed him with the spiritual grace of true recognition of Jesus. Thus baptism by water merely confirms a prior situation of baptism by fire and by spirit, the fire of the love of God and the spirit of life.[83] True baptism is not with material water at all—the thief on the cross was not baptised—and the baptism of infants is only a custom which is followed and has neither value nor significance.

Similarly with the eucharist: when Jesus, at the Last Supper, broke bread and passed it to the disciples and then passed round the Cup, he was clearly at that time complete and entire before them. He did not give them parts of Himself. His purpose was surely to call the disciples and through them His future followers to recollect Him—His new covenant with them, replacing the old covenant, His unbreakable bond with the faithful—and to help them so to do he asked them to recall the circumstances, just prior to His supreme sacrifice of martyrdom, by gathering at the love feast in His name. The recollection, the new covenant, had as its intention the assured continuance of the practice of His teachings, the following of His counsel and guidance, so that they might draw to themselves His perfections and thereby grow in spiritual stature towards the fuller reflection of the image of God. Through love of Him they would observe His commandments, His word, and attain the supreme human virtues and thereby fulfil the very purpose of their existence. The Last Supper was a social gathering, the occasion the most solemn, and the purpose to recall His covenant with His followers to love one another even as He had loved them, prepared to sacrifice even life itself for each other. The spiritual grace again preceded

40

the act. Again the sacrament of the eucharist today bears no resemblance to the original occasion.

Somewhat similarly with the sacrament of matrimony. The grace of God's joining together precedes the act of social recognition, the bridal couple are mutually attracted through God's grace or they are but drawn together by animal selection. The first kind of union is solemnised and indissoluble, whether or not a ceremony occurs and is confirmed in the marriage service to strengthen the foundations of society; the second kind is outside the operation of religion at all and is merely governed by the laws, practices and customs of the society to which the parties belong.

Chapter 5

NEGLECTED TEACHINGS OF CHRIST

Let us imagine, if we can, that we have with us an intelligent, well-educated man, say a citizen of classical Athens of the 5th century B.C., with a form of religious amnesia, who had never heard of any of the religions current today, and in particular knew nothing about any of the multitudinous denominations and sects of Christianity. Suppose that we introduce him to the four Gospels and then, when he has read them through alertly and attentively, to each of the principal Christian churches in turn. Suppose we then note some of his reactions. Should we not find that he would be frequently exclaiming at the inconsistency between the practices and the tenets of these churches and the clear meanings of the teachings of the Gospels, even though he might well acknowledge, with due humility, that brief acquaintance with the Gospels based on only two or three perusals, was inadequate to plumb the depth of meanings contained in those teachings?

Our imaginary Athenian, reading the Gospels in their original Greek as well as our modern English translations, might feel that his own pure language of some 500 or 600 years earlier had become altered and strained and put to strange uses by the authors of the Gospels. He would understand the Greek text fairly well, though he would be surprised to find that the English versions did not always accurately represent the Greek original because the languages are not at all points equally rich. He would remark that the word " master " represented no fewer than six different Greek words each with a distinct shade of meaning, that the word " judgement " in English was used to translate eight different Greek words and that the English " but " represented twelve different Greek words and he would notice many other such instances.

After inevitably reacting in this way to the textual differences, he might well be astounded to learn that scores of Christian churches, denominations and sects regarded any word in the English authorised or official version as infallibly accurate. What then is he to think of those nuances and shades of meaning contained in the many different Greek words in the original text from which the English version was translated? Is he to think the Greek text less accurate, although nearer the time of the authors themselves, than the later English version, or is he to think that changes had been introduced into the Greek test, the earliest extant copy of which is at least 300 years later than the death of the authors, between the original

42

authorship and that earliest copy, and that these changes had been corrected by persons during translation as a result of direct divine inspiration?

These surprises noted, our imaginary Athenian next turns to the official creeds of some of the churches, taking one of the simplest first—the ' Apostles Creed ', composed about 340 A.D., which he finds is accepted by a very large number of churches.

" I believe in God the Father Almighty, Maker of heaven and earth, and Jesus Christ His only Son, our Lord, who was conceived by the Holy Ghost, born of the Virgin Mary, suffered under Pontius Pilate, was crucified, dead and buried; He descended into hell; the third day He rose again from the dead; He ascended into heaven and sitteth on the right hand of God the Father Almighty; from thence He shall come to judge the quick and the dead;

" I believe in the Holy Ghost; the Holy Catholic Church; the communion of saints; the forgiveness of sins; the resurrection of the body, and the life everlasting ".

He would remark the beauty of the cadences in the version of the English Book of Common Prayer. But would he not wonder at the inclusion of certain points and the exclusion of others? Might he not take the stand that this creed, as other creeds, had been devised at a particular time in the development of Christianity, when certain points required emphasis, to the neglect of others, in order to counter the views and opinions (heresies) of certain unorthodox but attractive Christian groups or churches, even of certain non-Christian influences?

Points included which he might regard as deliberately selective might be:

1. " *His only Son, our Lord* ": What then of the words, " But as many as received him, to them gave he power to become the sons of God, even to them that believe on his name: which were born, not of blood, nor of the will of the flesh, nor of the will of man, but of God "?[1]

2. " *Who was conceived by the Holy Ghost* ": Other thoughts might also pass through our student's mind in regard to the origin of Adam without father or mother,[2] of Isaac[3] and of John the Baptist.[4] He might think that specially chosen people could be conceived simultaneously by human agency and by spiritual agency and that the important thing was the spiritual agency, that which singled them out from others.

3. " *Born of the Virgin Mary* ": It might cross his mind that any first child may be conceived of a virgin, that several times in the Gospels Jesus is referred to as the son of Joseph[5] through whom descent from the royal line of David consituted a considerable part of the recognition of the station of Jesus as the Jewish Messiah, both according to prophecy and according to the Gospels themselves.[6] He might be surprised that such stress is laid on the Virgin

birth especially as no great respect seemed to be paid to Adam who, according to the holy book of Genesis, was born without father or mother but out of the breath or spirit from God.

4. " *Dead* ": What, he thinks, of " This is the bread which cometh down from heaven that a man may eat thereof, and not die "?[7]

5. " *He descended into hell, the third day he rose again from the dead* ": Ringing in his ears are the words of Jesus from the death scene on the cross, addressed to the malefactor crucified beside him, " Verily, I say unto thee, today shalt thou be with me in paradise ".[8] He perhaps also recalls that from Friday afternoon to Sunday morning is less than two days.

6. " *He ascended into heaven* ": But Jesus never left heaven! " And no man hath ascended up to heaven, but he that came down from heaven, even the son of man which is in heaven ".[9]

7. " *From thence he shall come to judge the quick and the dead* ".

8. " *The Holy Catholic Church* ".

9. " *Resurrection of the body* ". " That which is born of the flesh is flesh,"[10] " For all flesh is as grass, and all the glory of man as the flower of grass. The grass withereth, and the flower thereof falleth away: but the word of the Lord endureth forever ",[11] " Wherefore, if God so clothes the grass of the field, which today is, and tomorrow is cast into the oven ".[12]

Our cultured Athenian might agree that the statements of the creed could be interpreted in an acceptable way so that they had truth, but why select these points—some of them so debatable—and overlook reference to other teachings surely of greater significance for an affirmation of sincere belief? Perhaps he might think, by the fourth century, emphasis had come to be placed on non-essentials because the community of believers was already shattered irretrievably and particular tenets were to be acknowledged because supported by the weight and power of numbers.

Was this all one needed to affirm to be acknowledged as a Christian before being subjected to the sacrament of baptism? What had become of the great community-building injunctions, the attitude-moulding exhortations? Where now were the pivotal words, Jesus new commandment, " that ye love one another; as I have loved you, that ye also love one another. By this shall all men know that you are my disciples if you have love one to another "?[13] What had become of his injunction: " Verily, I say unto you, Except ye be converted, and become as little children, ye shall not enter into the kingdom of heaven "?[14] or again of " Not every one that saith unto me, ' Lord, Lord!' shall enter into the kingdom of heaven, but he that doeth the will of my Father which is in heaven "?[15] or, " Whosoever therefore shall break one of these least commandments and shall teach men so, he shall be called the

44

least in the kingdom of heaven "?[16] or, " Put up again thy sword
into his place: for all they that take the sword shall perish with the
sword "?[17] or, " But I say unto you which hear, love your enemies,
do good to them which hate you, bless them that curse you, and
pray for them which despitefully use you "?[18]

The insistence on acknowledgement of a special creed surely
smacked of the same outlook as that of those to whom Jesus once
said, " The Sabbath is made for man, not man for the Sabbath ".[19]
or that of those he castigated, { Beware of the scribes, which love
to go in long clothing, and love salutations in the market place, and the
chief seats in the synagogues, and the uppermost rooms at feasts,
which devour widows' houses, and for a pretence make long
prayers ".[20]

Sadly our Athenian would conclude, what had promised so
gloriously, had spread so far and so effectively through the sacrifice
of so many precious lives, and had created such a wonderful
reciprocating community among the poor as to be the admiration
and inspiration of the great Greek physician, Galen, had now become
adulterated until mere conformity with the lips was enough. The
tree once so fresh and blooming had become corrupted and changed
or had reverted, until it could scarcely be distinguished from other
trees such as the barren fig tree which Jesus himself had cursed[21]
to indicate that at its religious centre the great religion of Moses
had become totally barren of fruit, and by so doing symbolically to
abrogate the dispensation or era of Moses.

Chapter 6

WHAT DID JESUS TEACH?

Several ways suggest themselves for determining the true content and purpose of the teachings of Jesus. In doing so we must beware the twin dangers of not seeing the wood for the individual trees or of seeing the trees of one particular type to the exclusion of other kinds. We also need to beware the erection of a sort of hierarchy of importance among the teachings unless we can show what different degrees of importance were clearly intended either by special emphasis, by reiteration or by other means.

Attention in the past has tended to be directed, perhaps unduly, to the environmental and descriptive setting of the teachings in a way which many think may have led to a misconception of, or at least a biassed weighting of, certain of the teachings, and to have caused an unnecessary sense of incompatibility with reason as a result of which so many of the people of today either accept blindly and unquestioningly what they are told, with all the risks of subsequent disillusion, or reject the whole religion of Christ because apparently inappropriate to an age of science.

In keeping with our declared intention we shall try to achieve our aim in six steps:—

1. Jesus' own purposes as stated by Himself.
2. Review of the Gospels.
3. Study of the actual precepts of Jesus, both positive and negative, so as to try to derive a coherent pattern.
4. Consideration of the parables and the miracles in the light of this pattern.
5. Examination of the result to see if it can be summarised and try to draw conclusions.
6. If necessary, examination of some problems and contradictory statements with an attempt to resolve them.

Jesus' own purposes as stated by Himself

Clearly relevant to the question, ' What did Jesus teach ?', are His own purposes as expressed by Himself in the Gospel. To an unbiassed reader it is remarkable the frequency with which He refers to His purposes in coming among men. Such references, either direct or indirect, are to be found at least 23 times in Matthew, 10 times in Mark, 17 times in Luke and 32 times in John. These 82 references can be classified into 19 different purposes.

The different purposes discerned are these, with one passage quoted against each. The full range of passages are set out in Appendix C.

1.   Primary purpose of Jesus' mission, to ' fish ' men, individual souls, from the sea of materialism, the world of nature.

> " Come ye after me, and I will make you to become fishers of men ".[1]

2.   To demonstrate the universality of His message, sowing the Word.

> " He that soweth the seed is the Son of man; the field is the world . . .".[2]

> " I must preach the kingdom of God to other cities also: for therefore am I sent ".[3]

3.   To renew the true religion of God, ' call not the righteous but sinners ', ' fulfil not destroy ', ' save the lost '.

> " For the Son of man is come to see and to save that which was lost ".[4]

4.   To free people from the past, and enable entrance into more abundant life.

> " And as Moses lifted up the serpent in the wilderness, even so must the Son of man be lifted up: that whosoever believeth in him should not perish, but have eternal life ".[5]

5.   To abrogate and alter.

> " For the Son of man is Lord even of the sabbath day ".[6]

6.   To precipitate reaction and bring about His own ultimate sacrifice.

> " The Son of man must suffer many things, and be rejected of the elders and chief priests and scribes, and be slain, and be raised the third day"'.[7]

7.   To demonstrate the station of servitude.

> " For even the Son of man came not to be ministered unto, but to minister, and to give his life a ransom for many ".[8]

8.   To fulfil promise and expectation, to bear witness to the truth.

> " The Son of man indeed goeth, as it is written of him: but woe to that man by whom the Son of man is betrayed . . .".[9]

9.   To announce the imminence of the kingdom of God, casting out devils by the spirit of God.

> " But if I cast out devils by the Spirit of God. then the kingdom of God is come unto you ".[10]

10.   To show the proper character of his true followers—sheep amid wolves, comfort of soul, knowledge of the doctrine, example, active teachers, mutual love, obedience to the Father's will, etc.

> " Ye have not chosen me, but I have chosen you, and ordained you, that ye should go and bring forth fruit, and that your fruit should remain: that whatsoever ye shall ask of the

Father in my name, he may give it you. These things I command you, that ye love one another ".[11]

11. To challenge existing patterns, to judge—

" Think not that I am come to send peace on earth: I came not to send peace, but a sword ".[12]

12. To reveal the Father and seek his glory.

" When ye have lifted up the Son of man, then shall ye know that I am he, and that I do nothing of myself; but as my Father hath taught me, I speak these things: and he that sent me is with me: the Father hath not left me alone; for I do always those things that please him ".[13]

13. To give the sign of the prophet Jonah, i.e. to demonstrate the truth of His Reality after a period of confusion and circumstances conducive to despair, to foretell His end, to safeguard His faith.

" Now I tell you before it come, that, when it is come to pass, ye may believe that I am he ".[14]

14. To conceal the truth from the unready, to speak in parables.

" Therefore speak I to them in parables: because they seeing see not; and hearing they hear not, neither do they understand. And in them is fulfilled the prophecy of Esaias, which saith, By hearing ye shall hear, and shall not understand; and seeing ye shall see, and shall not perceive: for this people's heart is waxed gross, and their ears are dull of hearing, and their eyes they have closed; lest at any time they should see with their eyes, and hear with their ears, and should understand with their heart, and should be converted, and I should heal them ".[15]

15. To warn of the leaven of the Pharisees, Sadducees and Herodians.

" How is it that ye do not understand that I spake it not to you concerning bread, that ye should beware of the leaven of the Pharisees and of the Sadducees?".[16]

16. To call first on the lost sheep of the house of Israel.

" Thus it is written, and thus it behoved Christ to suffer, and to rise from the dead on the third day: and that repentance and remission of sins should be preached in his name among all nations, beginning at Jerusalem "[17]

17. To redress injustices.

" The Spirit of the Lord is upon me, because he hath anointed me to preach the gospel to the poor; he hath sent me to heal the broken-hearted, to preach deliverance to the captives, and recovering of sight to the blind, to set at liberty them that are bruised, to preach the acceptable year of the Lord ".[18]

18.   To inaugurate His own remembrance and that of the perfection of the Spirit of God.

" For this is my blood of the new testament, which is shed for many for the remission of sins ".[19]

19.   To establish unity among His faithful followers, with Him, with the Father.

" Neither pray I for these alone, but for them also which shall believe on me through their word; that they all may be one; as thou, Father, art in me, and I in thee, that they also may be one in us: that the world may believe that thou has sent me. And the glory which thou gavest me I have given them; that they may be one, even as we are one: I in them, and thou in me, that they may be made perfect in one; and that the world may know that thou hast sent me, and hast loved them, as thou hast loved me. Father, I will that they also, whom thou hast given me, be with me where I am; that they may behold my glory, which thou hast given me: for thou lovedst me before the foundation of the world. O righteous Father, the world hath not known thee: but I have known thee, and these have known that thou hast sent me. And I have declared unto them thy name, and will declare it: that the love wherewith thou hast loved me may be in them, and I in them ".[20]

Some of the passages quoted, as may be seen, are virtually identical. Some of the passages illustrate more than one purpose. The 19 purposes thus distinguished can be grouped into six principal aims:

1.   To fulfil: no. 8
2.   To confirm or renew: no. 3
3.   To abrogate: no. 5
4.   To judge: nos. 6, 11, 17
5.   To initiate: nos. 1, 2, 4, 7, 10, 12, 13, 14, 15, 16, 17, 18, 19
6.   To herald: nos. 9, 12.

As befits the Harbinger of a new era among men, the greater number of His expressed purposes related to the inauguration of His own dispensation or age of spiritual authority over the hearts and souls of men.

Chapter 7

REVIEW OF THE GOSPELS

John's Gospel was by all accounts the latest of the four canonical Gospels to be written. It is usually attributed to about 100 A.D., some 70 years after the crucifixion and was therefore written at a time when the life of Jesus could be recollected in fuller perspective and the purpose of His glorious mission seen more clearly in the light of the slowly maturing fruits, than at the much earlier dates of the other, the synoptic Gospels.

Of the other three Gospels, the first to be written was that of Mark, while those of Matthew and Luke, written for different groups of people, incorporated nearly the whole of Mark and added material from a common but independent source. Each also included a few further items unique to itself.

The order of approach to this review of the Gospels should, for our purpose, be first to consider the Gospel of John, then that of Mark, and finally whatever is to be found in the Gospels of Matthew and Luke which does not appear in the other two Gospels. Attention will be almost exclusively focused on what Jesus actually said rather than on the setting or circumstances in which He said it.

Approach to an Evaluation

John's Gospel comprises only 21 chapters. Of its 879 verses (as set out in the Authorised Verson), 420, or slightly less than half, comprise or contain words of Jesus Himself. The actual incidents described are relatively few; they could all easily have taken place within a matter of a few weeks. Similarly, the miracles and parables recorded in this Gospel are few. The whole work leads up to the climax of the last supper to which five chapters, 13 to 17, are devoted. Other incidents are clearly important to have been selected at all from the much larger bulk of material that must have been available to the author (cf. 21:25), but the last supper and its injunctions are surely pre-eminent.

Emphasis in teaching may be inferred in a variety of ways:

i What is put first.

ii What is put last.

iii What is repeated several times, either in the same way or in a variety of ways.

iv What is specifically stated to be important.

   v What is emphasied in strong imperatives or in some other specially emphatic way.

   vi What is mentioned at a particularly selected and emphasised occasion.

What then are the injunctions and teachings of Jesus which the author of John's Gospel particularly emphasised in one or other of these six ways?

It will be convenient to list them first in the order in which they come in the book, noting which method of emphasis is used, and then try and combine them into a coherent whole. If this synthesis appears to be consistent in pattern it will be helpful then perhaps to review some of the problems that arise in other parts of the Gospel to see if they can be reconciled with the primary and fundamental teachings as they have emerged from our study. At that point we should be able to see John's Gospel as a whole and attempt an evaluation.

Primary Injunctions

John's Gospel in effect begins and ends with the words, " Follow me ", an injunction which is repeated three times in this Gospel; it appears three times in Mark's Gospel and five times and four times in Matthew's and Luke's Gospels respectively.[1] Between the first and last occasion on which these words are used the meaning is heightened and intensified immeasurably. The importance of this particular injunction cannot be over-emphasised, since no other injunction can have much meaning or weight until there is at least recognition and readiness to listen.

1.   " Come and see " (1:39) i.e. where Jesus lived, in reply to his first disciples, and " Follow me " (1:43) to Peter.

2. " Sin no more " (5:14), also in several other passages.[2]

3. " Be not afraid " (6:20), repeated twice elsewhere.[3]

4. " A new commandment I give unto you, That ye love one another; as I have loved you, that ye also love one another " (13:34), repeated five times in different ways.[4]

5. " Believe me that I am in the Father, and the Father in me: or else believe me for the very work's sake " (14:11)— Jesus many times speaks of His relations with His Father.[5]

6. " If ye love me, keep my commandments " (14:15), see also three other places.[6]

7. " Abide in me, and I in you " (15:4), repeated twice.[7]

8. " Remember the word that I said unto you, The servant is not greater than his lord " (15:20)—this was the second such reference.[8]

9. " Feed my sheep " (21:15), twice repeated.[9]

10. " Follow me " (21:22), as thrice before.[10]

51

Of all these emphatic instructions the most emphatic is the fourth. It is reiterated several times and each time the word " command " is used, the strongest imperative. It is surely right to infer that this is the keystone and heart of the message of Jesus, (especially as all the mentions also occur in the chapters on the last supper) that His followers love one another even as Jesus had loved them.

These injunctions may be rephrased perhaps in the following way:

' Investigate for yourselves and follow Me: detach yourselves from the bondage of your natural desires and do not be afraid: love one another even to giving your lives for one another: trust wholly in Me as one with full authority from God the Father: keep My commandments for love of Me: remain firm in your faith in Me: beware lest you set yourselves above Me (or join partners with God): feed My life-giving words to the receptive who await your guidance: follow My example '.

These do not exhaust the injunctions contained in John's Gospel, for there are many others of great importance. They will be taken up later.

Essential and Primary Teachings

The next degree of emphasis, after those specially emphatic injunctions, is surely that marked with the words, " verily, verily, I say unto you ", with which Jesus prefaces a number of statements. The passages concerned are these, again as they occur in the book:

1. " Hereafter ye shall see heaven open, and the angels of God ascending and descending upon the Son of man " (1:51).
2. " Except a man be born again, he cannot *see* the kingdom of God " (3:3), i.e. with ' blindness ' removed from inner vision.
3. " Except a man be born of water and of spirit, he cannot enter into the kingdom of God " (3:5).
4. " We speak that we do know, and testify that we have seen; and ye receive not our witness " (3:11).
5. " The Son can do nothing of himself, but what he seeth the Father do: for what things soever he doeth, these also doeth the son likewise " (5:19).
6. " He that heareth my word, and believeth on him that sent me, hath everlasting life, and shall not come into condemnation; but is passed from death unto life " (5:24).
7. " The hour is coming, and now is, when the dead shall hear the voice of the Son of God: and they that hear shall live " (5:25).
8. " Ye seek me, not because ye saw the miracles, but because ye did eat of the loaves, and were filled " (6:26).

52

9. " Moses gave you not that bread from heaven; but my Father giveth you the true bread from heaven " (6:32).

10. " He that believeth on me hath everlasting life " (6:47).

11. " Except ye eat the flesh of the Son of man, and drink his blood, ye have no life in you " (6:53).

12. " Whosoever committeth sin is the servant of sin " (8:34).

13. " If a man keep my saying, he shall never see death " (8:51).

14. " Before Abraham was, I am " (8:58).

15. " He that entereth not by the door into the sheepfold, but climbeth up some other way, the same is a thief and a robber " (10:1).

16. " I am the door of the sheep " (10:7).

17. " Except that a corn of wheat fall into the ground and die, it abideth alone: but if it die, it bringeth forth much fruit (12:24).

18. " The servant is not greater than his lord; neither is he that is sent greater than he that sent him " (13:16).

19. " He that receiveth whomsoever I send receiveth me; and he that receiveth me, receiveth him that sent me " (13:20).

20. " One of you shall betray me " (13:21).

21. " The cock shall not crow, till thou hast denied me thrice " (13:38).

22. " He that believeth on me, the works that I do shall he do also; and greater works than these shall he do; because I go to my father " (14:12).

23. " Ye shall weep and lament, but the world shall rejoice: and ye shall be sorrowful, but your sorrow shall be turned into joy " (16:20).

24. " Whatsoever ye shall ask the father in my name, he will give it you " (16:23).

The careful reader will note that some of these emphatic sayings are virtually repetitions of the same teaching in slightly different words. These may surely be regarded as the most important among them. Second birth is essential for the Kingdom of God (twice) for seeing it, for entering it, and must be by water and the spirit. Hearing and believing and obeying (" keeping my word ") Jesus and the Father leads to life, to everlasting life, to greater works, to being given whatever is asked; to fail to do so is to be " dead " for Jesus and the Father are identical in their deeds (cf. nos. 5, 6, 7 10, 11, 13, 19, 21, 23).

These teachings may perhaps be rephrased as follows:

' The inner eye of the pure-hearted shall be opened and he shall see and realise the true station of the Son of Man (Jesus); unless the inner being of man is turned again to the Source of Truth through the water of knowledge and the spirit of life he can

53

neither see (realise) nor enter the Kingdom of God; although We speak the real truth the hearts of men are still unreceptive; We speak and act with authority identical with that of God the Father; whoever, therefore, now ' dead ', hears (responds) and believes and obeys My words and therefore the words of God, shall live, have everlasting life, not see death, become attuned to the forces of life, not abide alone but produce much fruit, achieve great results, even greater than Mine, shall suffer but attain joy, shall be given whatever he asks of God; but the motive must be pure—the ' miracles ' must not be the cause, nor the mere eating of the ' loaves '; in the days of Moses the sustenance given, though material, came from God: now the sustenance that you must eat is not material and also came from the Father: you must ' eat ' of this intimately, really partake of the perfections, the ' flesh ' and the ' blood ', of the Son of man, to be a true believer. Sinful actions prove continued servitude to sin (to natural desires, to selfish, materialist, impure proclivities and instincts); My real station with God goes back long before Abraham, an immemorial authority; I am the door to life for My true followers: though there may be persons who seek to enter into My Kingdom by some other way they are in reality thieves and robbers; even My servants must beware lest they place themselves on a footing with Me, and therefore with Him that sent Me, and, by doing so and relying on their own intelligence, interpret God's message, steal its authority and take away its fruits, for those who hear them will suppose they hear Me and the Father who sent Me; even one of you present here shall betray Me; even the chief among you, Peter, shall deny Me thrice '.

Secondary Injunctions

Apart from these emphatic, primary and essential injunctions and teachings, there are several other occasions where Jesus used the imperative in John's Gospel. There are also several other teachings, some of which are almost as clearly emphasised as those just quoted.

The secondary injunctions, i.e. all the remaining imperatives used by Jesus, are these:

1. " Fill the waterpots with water . . . Draw out now and bear to the governor of the feast " (2:7-8).
2. " Take these things hence; make not my Father's house an house of merchandise " (3:16).
3. " Marvel not that I said unto thee, Ye must be born again " (3:7).
4. " Give me to drink . . . Go, call thy husband, and come hither " (4:7, 16).
5. " Behold, I say unto you, lift up your eyes, and look on the fields; for they are white already to harvest " (4:35).
6. " Go thy way; thy son liveth " (4:50).

7. " Rise, take up thy bed, and walk . . . Behold, thou art made whole: sin no more, lest a worse thing come unto thee " (5:8, 14).

8. " Search the scriptures; for in them ye think ye have eternal life: and they are they which testify of me . . . Do not think that I will accuse you to the Father: there is one that accuseth you, even Moses, in whom ye trust " (5:39, 45).

9. " Make the men sit down . . . Gather up the fragments that remain, that nothing be lost " (6:10, 12).

10. " Labour not for the meat which perisheth, but for that meat which endureth unto everlasting life, which the Son of man shall give unto you: for him has God the Father sealed " (6:27).

11. " Murmur not among yourselves " (6:43).

12. " Go ye up unto the feast: I go not up yet unto this feast; for my time is not yet come " (7:8).

13. " Judge not according to the appearance, but judge righteous judgement " (7:24).

14. " Go, wash in the pool of Siloam " (9:7).

15. " Take ye away the stone . . . Lazarus, come forth . . . Loose him, and let him go " (11:39, 43, 44).

16. " Let her alone: against the day of my burying hath she kept this " (12:7).

17. " That thou doest, do quickly " (13.27).

18. " Arise, let us go hence " (14:31).

19. " I have told you that I am he: if therefore ye seek me, let these go their way " (18:8).

20. " Put up thy sword into the sheath: the cup which my Father hath given me, shall I not drink it?" (18:11).

21. " Why askest thou me? Ask those which heard me, what I have said unto them; behold, they know what I said . . . If I have spoken evil, bear witness of the evil: but if well, why smitest thou me?" (18:21, 23).

22. " Woman, behold thy son! . . . Behold thy mother!" (19:26, 27).

23. " Touch me not; for I am not yet ascended unto my Father: but go to my brethren, and say unto them, I ascend unto my Father; and to my God, and your God " (20:17).

24. " Reach hither thy finger, and behold my hands; and reach hither thy hand, and thrust it into my side: and be not faithless, but believing " (20:27).

25. " Cast the net on the right side of the ship, and ye shall find . . . Bring of the fish which ye have now caught . . . Come and dine " (21:6, 10,12).

As will have been noticed, where the imperatives relate to the same incident or occasion, they have been grouped together.

Some of these imperatives appear to be linked to a specific occasion rather than to have a general application, though the occasion itself must have had a special relevance to the purpose of the Gospel's author for it to have been selected for inclusion at all. Some of the imperatives seem to concern the general framework of the life of Jesus which is less carefully described than in the other Gospels but nevertheless provides a beginning, middle and end to the account. Some of the imperatives illustrate special attributes of Jesus such as compassion or sense of justice.

Yet it seems possible to rephrase nearly all of them so that they carry a general application. These injunctions or imperatives are of five different kinds—

1. Challenge to standard orthodox Judaism which had become parched, dried up, materialistic, dead, yet must be conformed to.

2. New life resulting from His creative life-giving mission.

3. Warnings and advice to those just discovering the truth, to his followers.

4. Illustration of specific attributes of Jesus in action which should be practised also by His followers.

5. Dealing with incredulity.

Taking each of these in turn we can paraphrase as follows, with the particular quotations shown numbered in brackets.

1. *Challenge of Judaism.* The water of life conveyed through the former religion represented by the waterpots at the marriage feast, had dried up or lost its refreshing value (1). The effect of Jesus' presence was to give fresh invigorating life which was first felt by the master of ceremonies (1). The holy of holies of the religion, symbolised by the temple, had become desecrated, commercialised and must be cleansed (2). New spiritual awareness was necessary and none should be surprised at this in view of the decline of behaviour and subservience to natural desires and interests (3). The understanding of the purpose of the mission and teachings of Moses would clearly prove the truth of Jesus' own mission and condemn the orthodox Jews (8). One must not rely on outward superficial evidence, but be truly just in attitude and action (13). Even a loved brother of true believers may be dead, dyed in prejudice and perversity, so that it is especially hard to reach him and take away the barriers and veils (15). Yet conformity with the teachings of Judaism is to be practised including attendance at the feast, though not necessarily in a public kind of way (12), and proving freedom from disease after cure (14).

2. *New life at hand.* The easy receptivity of the people of Samaria (i.e. Gentiles) is made clear (4) and the fact that the people at large are ready for gathering into His following (5), even perhaps

not far, in the perspective of earth's history, from full maturity (5). Faith in Jesus confers life even for unbelievers, even at a distance (6). Freedom from sin, from the comfortable bed of bad habits, is needed for activity, but once roused there can be relapse and worse disillusion or worse results (7). Things pertaining to this vain, passing show, this worldly life, are not to be compared with things pertaining to eternity, the things of true life (10).

3. *Warnings and advice.* The feeding by the disciples of the multitude using the bread of life given by Jesus led to diverse interpretations or fragmentation of that bread of life, the Word; Jesus insisted that none be wasted, but all gathered together again (9). His disciples must live in harmony and not criticise one another or gossip (11). They must avoid violence to gain their ends even if the end is a good one (20). If unsuccessful in their search for responsive souls by one method or in one direction, they should rely on Jesus and try another (25).

4. *Illustration of Jesus' attributes.* If someone dedicates himself to a particular purpose linked with doing good, one should encourage it whatever it be; it can always be turned to good account and deserves praise (16). We should take our responsibilities on our own shoulders and not involve others unnecessarily (19). We should resign ourselves to our lot and make the most of it (20). We need to be just to ourselves also and require just action in others; proof of accusation and wrongdoing is needed before condemnation and punishment (21). We must be compassionate and loving towards those who are deprived of their own loved ones, treating them according to age and sex, as if they were near relations (22). We should be hospitable when we can (25).

5. *Dealing with incredulity.* By vividness of impression, by reminder of the familiar, by repeating what we have said before— the historical Jesus is a vivid, living fact, clear in every detail, to the eye of insight based on faith and belief (23 and 24). (The contradiction between 'Touch me not' and 'Reach hither thy finger' clearly implies that a spiritual meaning, not a literal one, is to be sought).

The only two imperatives not put to comment seem to be either too specific (17) or too unimportant (18) to warrant it.

The Last Supper

No less than five (chapters 13 to 17) of the twenty-one chapters of John's Gospel are devoted to the Last Supper. Clearly, the author of the gospel intended the Last Supper to be the heart and centre of the glad tidings he conveyed. Special attention should therefore be directed to the teachings those chapters contain.

Seven of the ten injunctions that we have suggested as primary occur in these chapters, four of them in these chapters only. More than one quarter of the teachings which are prefaced with the words

" Verily, verily, I say into you ", appear in these chapters. Let us review these again, first the seven injunctions:

1. " Sin no more ", or rather in the context (15: 14-24), " They (i.e. the people of the world), have both seen and hated both me and my Father " and are shown up in their sin: you, as true believers, " because ye are not of the world " will " go and bring forth fruit " and " your fruit shall remain " " if ye do whatsoever I command you " (cf. 15: 3)

2. " Be not afraid ", " let not your heart be troubled: ye believe in God, believe also in me " (14: 1, also 14: 27 and 16: 33)

3. " A new commandment I give unto you, that ye love one another ", a commandment repeated in different ways at least six times.

4. " Believe me ".

5. " Keep my commandments ", repeated at least three times in these chapters.

6. " Abide in me, and I in you ".

7. " Remember . . . the servant is not greater than his lord." and the six emphasised teachings:

8. " The servant is not greater than his lord."

9. " He that receiveth whomsoever I send receiveth me ".

10. " One of you shall betray me."

11. " He that believeth on me, the works that I do shall he do also."

12. " Ye shall weep and lament . . . but your sorrow shall be turned into joy."

13. " Whatsoever ye shall ask the Father in my name, he will give it you."

Other principal teachings contained in these chapters may be listed:

14. " Ye ought to wash one another's feet." (13: 14)

15. " Thou shalt follow me afterwards." (13: 36)

16. " In my Father's house are many mansions." (14: 2)

17. " I will come again, and receive ye unto myself . . ." (14: 3)

18. " I am the way, the truth and the life: no man cometh unto the Father, but by me." (14: 6)

19. " The Father that dwelleth in me, he doeth the works." (14: 10)

20. " If ye shall ask anything in my name, I will do it." (14: 14)

21. " And I will pray the Father, and he shall give you another Comforter, that he may abide with you for ever: even the Spirit of truth." (14: 16-17, cf. 14: 26, 15: 26, 16: 7, 16: 12-16, 16: 23)

22. " Peace I leave with you, my peace I give unto you " (14: 27)

23. " The prince of this world cometh " (14: 30, cf. 16: 11)

24. " I am the true vine, and my Father is the husbandman (15: 1) . . . Ye are the branches." (15: 5)

25. " Greater love hath no man than this, that a man lay down his life for his friends." (15: 13)

26. " Ye are my friends, if ye do whatsoever I command you." (15: 14)

27. " And you also shall bear witness, because ye have been with me from the beginning." (15: 27)

28. " Whosoever killeth you will think that he doeth God service." (16: 2)

29. " I have yet many things to say unto you, but you cannot bear them now, Howbeit when he, the Spirit of Truth, is come, he will guide you into all truth." (16: 12)

30. " In that day ye shall ask me nothing." (16: 23)

31. " Be of good cheer: I have overcome the world." (16: 33)

A number of these are almost identical with one another, a number are puzzling for their difference. It seems that they were recorded as recollected and, like the cryptic sayings in the Book of Daniel, were not meant to be understood until the seal was broken. These puzzles and problems we can look at later. The teachings of these crucial four chapters can perhaps be rephrased and summarised to make them clearer.

' I have chosen you out, indeed from the beginning you have been so selected, and you have become My friends (26) and know My way (18); you are clean, but the people of the world are shown up for their sins (1). You must put away fear (2) for I have conquered the world (31) and given you My peace within you (22), not of this world. You will be persecuted (12, 15), and people will even think they are doing God's work in persecuting you (28), but you will find the sadness and the pain turn into joy (12). You must believe Me (4), hold fast to My way, obey My commandments (5) for love of Me if you would continue to be My friends (13): especially must you love one another even to the point of sacrificing life for each other (3, 25). If you stand firm in this (6) you shall achieve mighty results (11), greater in scope than I Myself have achieved, but you must realise that just as it is God who is the true cause of My works (19), because We are identical in purpose, aim and spirit, so I will be the true cause of your results and shall give you whatever you ask in My name (13, 20). God sent Me and is greater than I (24). I send you and am greater than you (24). Beware lest you add to what I give you and make yourselves My equals (7, 8), but in all humility and love be concerned to remove from one another every defilement, every hindrance, every blemish (14).

'I know well that among you is one who will betray Me—let him act quickly (10).

'You are too immature now to be able to receive My whole message (29). Unhappily also, even the chief among you will deny Me three times before the dawn of the new day. I will send another (21) and I will come Myself (17) and the Spirit of Truth will come (29): each time I shall be honoured. When the Spirit of Truth comes you shall be led to all truth (29); at that time you will no longer need to ask in My name (30), but in His. for He will be the Prince of this world (23) and abide with you for ever (21).'

Jesus' Prayer

Just after the account of the Last Supper and just before the betrayal leading to trial and execution, there is a whole chapter (no. 17) comprising the only extensive prayer, or commune, recorded of Jesus in the entire range of the gospels. We cannot know how it came to be recorded, but its position in the book is of greatest significance. His work was at an end and all that remained, the inevitable, glorious, indispensable crown of martyrdom by crucifixion, would not be fruitful unless He had sufficiently completed His mission and achieved the necessary response for its further growth.

This prayer therefore deserves the most careful attention.

The 26 verses contain certain recurrent keynotes (numbers in brackets refer to verses):

1. " The hour is come " (1), " I have finished the work which thou gavest me to do " (4), " And now I am no more in the world " (11), " And now I come to thee " (13), " And for their sakes I sanctify myself " (19).

2. " Glorify thy son, that thy son also may glorify thee " (1), " I have glorified thee on earth " (4), " And now, O Father, glorify thou me with thine own self with the glory which I had with thee before the world was " (5), " And all mine are thine, and thine are mine; and I am glorified in them " (10), " And the glory which thou gavest me I have given them: that they may be one, even as we are one " (21), " Father, I will that they also . . . may behold my glory, which thou hast given me: for thou lovedst me before the foundation of the world " (24).

3. " As thou hast given him (thy Son) power over all flesh, that he should give eternal life to as many as thou hast given him " (2), " I have manifested thy name unto the men which thou gavest me out of the world: thine they were, and thou gavest them me; and they have kept thy word " (6), " I pray for them: I pray not for

the world, but for those which thou hast given me: for they are thine " (9), " Holy Father, keep through thine own name those whom thou hast given me " (11), " While I was with them in the world, I kept them in thy name; those that thou gavest me I have kept " (12), " and these things I speak in the world, that they might have my joy fulfilled in themselves " (13), " I have given them thy word; and the world hath hated them, because they are not of the world, even as I am not of the world " (14), " I pray not that thou shouldest take them out of the world, but that thou shouldest keep them from the evil " (15), " They are not of the world, even as I am not of the world " (16), " that the world may know that thou hast sent me, and hast loved them, as thou hast loved me " (23).

4. " And this is life eternal, that they might know thee the only true God, and Jesus Christ whom thou hast sent " (3), " Sanctify them through thy truth; thy word is thy truth " (17).

5. " Neither pray I for these alone, but for those also which shall believe on me through their word " (20).

6. " That they all may be one; as thou, Father, art in me, and I in thee, that they also may be one in us: that the world may believe that thou hast sent me " (21), " that they may be one, even as we are one " (22), " I in them, and thou in me, that they may be made perfect in one " (23), " And I have declared unto them thy name, and will declare it: that the love wherewith thou hast loved me may be in them, and I in them " (26).

These six themes overlap and do not exhaust the content of this so moving prayer. Yet they do illustrate perfectly the theme of the entire gospel which may be repeated in different words:

' God, the Father, selected Jesus Christ for a special redemptive mission among men. In God's method there is no change, for He has always made such a selection to mediate His word, His will, from the beginning of time: the Mediator changes name and personality, but His essence is the same and His message is the same: in relation to men the intermediary is as God, identical with the will of God, born of God's spiritual substance; in relation to God He is a receptive vehicle or instrument, wholly obedient and completely self-sacrificing. Those who respond do so because they too are selected by God, the Father; they receive eternal life because of their response. There is always the exception who responds, believes and then betrays and is lost. Entry into life eternal depends on response to God and His appointed intermediary, and continuing to believe, to obey, to love Him and to be detached from the world; it also means for the believers to be at one with each other. The world will be out of touch with God, unaware of Him; failing to recognise His intermediary it will hate those who respond, obey, accept and love both God, his intermediary and each other. They who respond and believe therefore need protection against temptation lest they become again contaminated by the world, as was the case with the betrayer. Those who come to believe later must maintain the same standard of response, detachment, obedience, love and oneness with each other, sustaining these through the name and word of God and His intermediary, His Messenger. The Messenger Himself will inevitably suffer condemnation and persecution, but will thereby achieve glory and return to God, the Father, whence He was sent.

His followers, loving Him, will also face self-sacrifice on the road to glory, to spiritual joy and the limitless heights and depths of the love of God.'

Mark's Gospel—Injunctions of Jesus

In Mark's Gospel there are 128 imperatives used, commandments of the most high God delivered through His chosen Messenger to man. Well over half of these were addressed to the disciples as themselves individually, or collectively, as representatives of the Christian community destined to come into being after them or as representatives of mankind at large; nearly one third were addressed to individuals on occasions either specific to themselves or as appropriate for general guidance; a number (11) concerned ratification of the commandments of God delivered to man through Moses; a few were directed as challenges to His opponents, the scribes and Pharisees; a few constituted demonstrations of His unusual powers. A particular injunction in Mark's Gospel which should be noted is that in which the almost equivalent words ' Watch ', ' Take heed ', ' Beware ', occur 13 times, as if this were the most important thing that Christ wished to impress upon His hearers, His disciples, and as if they were in great danger of failing to do just that.

To mankind at large

In order as they come in the gospel the imperatives addressed to mankind at large as these:

" *Repent* ye and *believe* the gospel " (1: 15)

" *Hearken; behold,* there went out a sower to sow " (4: 3)

" *Hearken* unto me every one of you, and *understand* " 7: 14)

" Whosoever will come after me, *let him deny himself,* and *take up his cross,* and *follow me* " (8: 34)

" *No man eat* fruit of thee hereafter for ever " (11: 14)

" *Beware* of the scribes, which love to go in long clothing, and love salutations in the market places, and the chief seats in the synagogues, and the uppermost rooms at feasts: which devour widows' houses, and for a pretence make long prayers: these shall receive greater damnation " (12: 38-40)

" And what I say unto you I say unto all, *Watch* " (13: 37)

The general pattern of the message is surely clear indeed: Repent—believe—hearken—understand—deny self—take up personal burdens—follow—seek sustenance no longer from the figtree (Judaism)—beware—watch. These ten vital injunctions can be rephrased: Turn away from disobedience and obey God's call: believe the good news I bring; listen to Me; understand My words carefully; try to master your selfish inclinations, to face manfully the burdens of life, to follow My example; the religion of Moses has no more life in it; look out for the intellectual and hypocritical religious leaders; be vigilant or you will be led astray.'

To the disciples, His associates and future custodians of His message

The chosen few were clearly to be the key figures in the religion of God which Christ came to renew. Unless they believed, understood, had faith, followed, practised, all would be lost. The injunctions they received were therefore more numerous, more detailed, of deeper import, more strongly couched:

" *Come* ye after me, and I will make you to become fishers of men " (1: 17)

" *Follow* me " (2: 14)

" *Behold* my mother and my brethren!" (3: 34)

" *Take heed what ye hear:* with what measure ye mete, it shall be measured to you " (4: 24)

" In what place soever ye enter into an house, there *abide* till ye depart from that place. And whosoever shall not receive you, nor hear you, when ye depart thence, *shake off* the dust under your feet for a testimony against them " (6: 10-11)

" *Come* ye yourselves *apart* into a desert place, and *rest* awhile " (6: 31)

" *Give* ye them *to eat* " (6: 37)

" How many loaves have ye? *Go and see* " (6: 35)

" *Be of good cheer:* It is I: *be not afraid* " (6: 50)

" *Take heed, beware* of the leaven of the Pharisees, and of the leaven of Herod " (8: 15)

" *Get thee behind* me, Satan " (8: 33)

" *Forbid him not:* for there is no man which shall do a miracle in my name, that can lightly speak evil of me " (9: 39)

" And if thy hand offend thee, *cut it off* " (9: 43)

" And if thy foot offend thee, *cut it off* " (9: 45)

" And if thine eye offend thee, *pluck it out* " (9: 47)

" *Have salt* in yourselves, and *have peace* with one another " (9: 50)

" *Suffer* the little children to come unto me, and *forbid them not;* for of such is the kingdom of God " (10: 14)

" *Go your way* into the village over against you: and as soon as ye be entered into it, ye shall find a colt tied, whereon never man sat, *loose him.* And if any man say unto you, ' Why do ye this?'

Say ye that the Lord hath need of him; and straightway he will send him hither " (11: 2-3)

" *Have faith* in God " (11: 22)

" Therefore I say unto you, what things soever ye desire, when ye pray, *believe* that ye receive them, and ye shall have them " (11: 24)

" And when ye stand praying, *forgive*, if ye have ought against any " (11: 24)

" *Take heed* lest any man deceive you " (13: 5)

" And when ye shall hear of wars and rumours of wars, *be ye not troubled* " (13: 7)

" But *take heed* to yourselves . . ." (13: 9)

" But when they shall lead you, and deliver you up, *take no thought* beforehand, what ye shall speak, *neither do ye premeditate:* but whatsoever shall be given you, in that hour, that *speak ye*, for it is not ye that speak, but the Holy Ghost " (13: 11)

" But when ye shall see the abomination of desolation spoken of by Daniel the prophet, standing where it ought not, (let him that then readeth understand), and *let* them that be in Judaea *flee* to the mountains: and *let* him that is on the house top *not go down* into the house, *neither enter* therein, to take anything out of his house; and *let* him that is in the field *not turn back* for to take up his garment (13: 14-16)

" And *pray ye* that your flight be not in the winter " (13:18)

" And then, if any man shall say unto ye, ' Lo, here is Christ or, lo, he is there ': *believe him not* " (13: 21)

" But *take ye heed:* behold, I have foretold you all things " (13: 23)

" Now *learn* a parable of the figtree; when her branch is yet tender, and putteth forth leaves, ye know that summer is near. So ye in like manner, when ye shall see these things come to pass, *know* that it is nigh, even at the doors " (13: 28-29)

" *Take ye heed, watch and pray:* for ye know not when the time is " (13: 33)

" *Watch ye* therefore " (13: 35)

" *Let her alone:* why trouble ye her?" (14: 6)

" *Go ye into* the city, and there shall meet you a man bearing a pitcher of water: *follow* him. And wheresoever he shall go in, *say* ye to the good man of the house, ' The Master saith, " Where is the guest-chamber where I shall eat the passover with my disciples!' " And he will show you a large upper room furnished and prepared: there *make ready* for us " (14: 13-15)

" *Take, eat:* this is my body " (14: 22)

" My soul is exceeding sorrowful unto death: *tarry ye here* and watch " (14: 34)

" *Watch ye*, and pray, lest ye enter into temptation. The spirit truly is willing, but the flesh is weak " (14: 38)

" *Sleep on* now, and *take your rest* " (14: 41)

" *Rise up, let us go* " (14: 42)

" *Go ye into* all the world and *preach* the gospel to every creature " (16: 15)

Several features of this list of injunctions will have struck the careful reader. All but 16 of the 65 or so imperatives are from the second half of the book, as though Christ felt able to be increasingly stringent and imperative as the disciples came to realise His true mission and purpose, or as if the nearer the end came the more urgent He felt He had to be.

Two of the passages, those concerning the colt and the guest-chamber, seem to be slightly out of character or incongruous. It has been suggested that they were inserted because they had a special connection with the writer of the gospel himself, or with his own family. They can also be taken as indicating special precognition on the part of Christ, or pre-arrangement made by Him independently of the disciples; or again they may be quoted to indicate the compelling power of the divine will which ultimately possesses anything it requires.

Then there is a whole series of passages, 11 of them, in which Christ is clearly addressing the disciples as representing those who are to come after them, since He refers to events, admittedly in a deliberately obscure manner, of the far distant future.

A further remarkable feature is the repetition. When taken together with His injunctions to mankind at large, which includes the disciples, " Take heed ", " Beware ", occurs 8 times,[11] " Watch "[12] occurs 5 times, " Come after " or " Follow me " occurs 3 times,[13] " Pray " occurs 3 times,[14] " Believe " (or " Have Faith in God ") occurs 3 times,[15] " Cut it off " (or " Pluck it out ") occurs 3 times.[16]

These injunctions to the disciples might be re-phrased and summarised:

' Follow My example and heed My words, become as near to Me as My closest relatives and win the hearts of men from the sea of materialism that surrounds them; beware of gossip and back-biting for you will suffer proportionately if you listen; leave those alone who will not listen to you, and have nothing more to do with them; freely feed the many who hunger for the Word of God; I shall be with you, so do not fear, however fierce the storm; look out for the influence of hypocritical officialdom and those who have worldly authority, as they can so easily contaminate your principles; do not attempt to thwart the purposes of God; do not prevent the good work of those who sympathise with our aims, even though they may not be of your own company; but reject anyone of yourselves, even one of high position and influence, if he be the cause of ' offence ', of serious obstruction to your life-giving work; above all be at peace and united with one another; the children of today are the citizens of tomorrow, let My teachings strengthen their innocent guilelessness so that the kingdom of God may well be founded; rely upon God and He will grant your needs when you pray, but before you pray, forgive, harbour no negative thought about anyone, beware deception, do not concern yourselves with the outer world of conflict, even if you are brought to severe trial; speak freely with faith, without prior preparation and you will be assisted; at the time of the end (when Daniel's prophecy is fulfilled) there will be great troubles—flee to the hills empty-handed and pray that the event takes place in summer; take no notice of people calling themselves Christians who claim authority to expound Christ, for they are false; when the ancient tree of religion shows life again, then the fruit season of summer is near, but stay alert and vigilant; and pray, and be very careful for you do not know when the great day will come; even though someone of their whole heart makes sacrifice of great value for love of Me, do not prevent it; hold regular remembrance feasts for Me, when you will by faith, mutuality and love draw your heavenly sustenance from the perfections of My spirit and My real being; be wakeful and pray that you may fully experience all that happens to Me; I know that you are not ready, are too immature still, so take your slumber; awaken yourselves; go out and tell the glad tidings to everyone everywhere.'

To Individuals

The injunctions Christ addressed to individuals are of three kinds. There are those which are related as being addressed to influences—spirits, possessing deluded or misguided persons. In such cases, where perhaps the tests of life have been too great for the retention of a stable mind, or where perhaps the conflict between deeply ingrained religion and the condition of the world around them or the shallow pretentiousness of the orthodox practitioners has temporarily shaken the personality from its firm foundation and instilled doubts and permitted pernicious influences, Christ offers definiteness, strength, freedom from guilt of the past—" Come out ", " Hold thy peace ", " Be thou clean ", " Enter no more ".

Then there are those cases of healing, of the palsy, of a withered arm, of an issue of blood, of apparent death, of deafness, of blindness. Again Christ uses sharp, positive action words to arouse and stimulate, often combined with symbolic actions of contrast: " Arise—Take up thy bed—Go thy way: Stand forth—stretch forth thy hand: Go in peace, and be whole: Be not afraid, only believe—Arise: Let the children first be filled—Be opened: Go thy way—thy faith hath made thee whole." The sense of inadequacy, of diffidence, of uncertainty, of hopelessness, of lack of insight, in each case is successfully challenged by forthright memorable positive action and words. In all such cases, except one, the individuals are charged to keep silent: Christ did not want the reputation of a miracle-worker as it would have attracted people for the wrong reasons. In one instance, that of someone living on the other side of the lake, an alien to the Jews, Christ wanted publicity since otherwise it might be a long time before the people of those parts had the chance to hear of His message.

The third kind of injunction occurred with the rich young man who said he had obeyed the laws of Moses from his youth and wanted to know what more he should do. Christ seemed to have perceived a tendency to complacency and challenged him to discard his ' props ', sell his possessions and live as His followers. This has been by some supposed to be autobiographical and about Mark himself; if so the injunction proved most effective, even though not at once.

To His enemies

Of the remaining imperatives in Mark's Gospel four are addressed to the critical challengers, the scribes and Pharisees, who tried to catch Him out with trick questions. They provided the opportunity for Christ to make some very explicit statements about His precepts. " What God hath joined together, let no man put asunder " (10: 9) in the context clarifies the right attitude to marriage: where marriage is based upon the bonds of attraction centred in eternal qualities there is no right of divorce. The precept clearly has wider connotations and may be taken as applicable wherever a spiritual unity created by God is concerned: any subsequent division or disunity can only be man-made, opposed to the divine intention and liable to attract the appropriate penalty.

" The baptism of John, was it from heaven, or of man? Answer me " (11:30) is a counterthrust trenchantly challenging the sincerity of His opponents. Authority is the basis of religion, divine authority. Unless there is clear willingness to acknowledge this, no useful purpose is served by discussing authority at all.

" Render to Caesar the things that are Caesar's, and to God the things that are God's " (12: 17) makes clear the duty of obedience to authority. Although some have taken it as permitting dual morality, to keep two different spheres of action and behaviour, this is surely wrong. If Christ had not meant obedience to authority, He would not have enjoined it—the same behaviour, the same virtue is clearly stipulated. It is at this stage too that Christ reaffirms and summarises the commandments of God given through Moses (12: 29-31): an attitude of love for God expressed through a life of love to one's neighbours.

The one remaining command is addressed to the elements, " Peace, be still " (14: 39). No matter what storms arise in the world or in life, Christ can and will enforce calm.

Chapter 8

PARABLES

In a restricted sense a parable is a vivid illustration of a spiritual truth by means of a story couched in everyday terms and simple language. The parable of the sower[1] is a good example from among many. In a more general sense a parable is another word for a vivid metaphor, e.g. " Ye are the salt of the earth ".[2] These senses of the word cannot be separated: " But without a parable spake he not unto them ".[3]

The parables were a mode of teaching used by Jesus for a number of reasons. Being vivid they lent themselves to accurate recollection, an important factor for a faith which was not recorded at its time of origination and indeed was not to be recorded for about a generation. Then the majority of those He addressed may well have been relatively, if not wholly, uneducated and simple people, and such were to form the bulk of His followers for hundreds of years. Jesus Himself said that He spoke in that way so that people for the most part should grasp His truth only at a literal level, while He reserved the deeper levels of meaning for His closer followers.

There are at least 94 parables in the Gospels, taking both senses of the term and disregarding repetition, of which 38 occur in Matthew, 7 in Mark, 44 in Luke and 5 in John. A list of them is given in Appendix D.

Perhaps only one of the parables is specific to Christianity in its meaning, viz. that of " destroy this temple, and in three days I will raise it up ".[4] The remaining parables express truths that could have been expressed equally well by Buddha, or Muhammad, though, of course, since their missions were different and they came at different times among different peoples, they expressed their teachings in different ways.

These parables each vividly illustrate a particular truth and all are of two general kinds (a) those which relate to the renewal of faith and religion (b) those that relate to the impending establishment of the kingdom of God.

What then are the teachings that Jesus sought to convey by the means of parable? The following is an attempt to present these teachings of the parables in a connected coherent statement linking them all together, the contribution of each parable being shown

68

by a numbered reference which can be checked against the list in Appendix D.

The Son of Man, Founder of His Faith, went forth to spread the Word of God, freely disseminating it over all the earth and meeting with different types of response, varying from total indifference to warm and ready embrace, with results appropriate to the response.[1] You who make the full response are a specially privileged people who must not keep the great gift of the Word of God and your faith to yourselves, but radiate it widely[2] so as to illuminate the whole world.[3] You must demonstrate such a unity, love and harmony among yourselves as to generate a sense of vital purpose in all you meet,[4] showing this by taking infinite pains to help any one of your number who may stray or be in difficulties. [5-6] You need to be chaste, unselfish, seeing no evil,[7] to be detached from the attractive rewards that this world has to offer,[8] to overlook weakness or defects in others for fear your own defects will challenge attention,[9] to be firmly rooted in the Word of God as the only sure foundation for life,[10] to maintain a joyous outlook rejoicing in life's fullness.[11] You need to act without reservation, delay or hypocrisy in accordance with God's will,[12] to sacrifice even that which lies most dear to you for the sake of spreading the faith.[13] Although the people of the world will be against you and will seek to destroy you[14] you will have a devastating effect on the outworn and outmoded conventions and customs which will not be able to resist the force of your vital message.[15-16] You will see everyone you meet as a potential focus of your loving attention and service.[17] The work before you is stupendous and will call for all your energy.[18] You will be assisted in all your requirements to follow the path of God.[19] You must beware of anyone in your own ranks who obstructs your progress and cast him out if need be, however important a member;[20] you must remember that all evil is from within man and can bring him low[21] and that absence of evil is not enough for it needs to be replaced with positive dynamic good or far worse will befall.[22] With all these points clear before you, you will become a life giving community of people with wonderful fruits shown forth by the civilisation you will create;[23] you will see religion reinstated as the chief bastion of society.[24] The people of the world, i.e. worldly people, lacking spiritual insight, are destined for utter loss and failure[25] and should be left to themselves[26] as there are plenty of others to seek out.[17] The religious leaders especially are to be watched for they are the focal centres of death, though seeming otherwise.[27] Rich people rarely, if ever, can respond to the message;[28] they receive their reward here on earth but compensate for this in the next world;[29] they tend to become immersed in their riches, complacent and self-satisfied.[30] The sincere man, regardless of his profession, is to be preferred to the conformist, the imitator, the self-important.[31] Often the worst sinner will make the best associate and worker for the cause, out of gratitude.[32] Nevertheless, you will need to live in the world, so you must always show forth at all times every good quality since, no matter what effort you display, you will not match the bounty of your Creator; showing loyalty in little matters proves the quality of soul, but you must beware to keep yourselves detached from the power of the world,[33] give your all without holding back,[34] maintaining complete solidarity[35] and remembering always that you are organically one with me and through me with the Father.[36]

Nevertheless, the people of my dispensation are immature, easily distracted, and tend to encourage others to do the work rather than to do it themselves.[37] Hence it is that I must tell you about the coming Kingdom of God of the future. The Kingdom of God is a naturally growing thing[38] that will permeate the whole world[39] and overshadow all on earth.[40] There will be a testing time at its inauguration when the Son of Man, returning[41] to His own in the person (identical in spiritual essence) of the Lord of Hosts, will test and gather to Himself the faithful and destroy the ungodly,[42] especially those He has trusted to supervise and safeguard His true faith whom He has found wanting,[43] for He will call all His servants (all people) at that time to account,[44] and will apply a consistent and undating test to all in the past or in the present,[45] embracing all without distinction in His assessment,[46] rewarding equally for faithful consistent service obedient to His will.[47] He will at that time invite all to enter but will find the established people of riches and property too engrossed in their worldly interests to respond so He will exercise compulsive attraction on the ordinary folk, as many of them as are sincere believers,[48-49] for rich people find it hard to respond due to their heavy preoccupation with the world's goods.[50] At that time the wise who have kept their faith pure,[51] have conscientiously maintained their standards of service,[52] who have made the most of their personal spiritual endowment,[53-54] will be distinguished by acceptance and admission from the foolish and faithless, the evil and ungodly, the improvident and indifferent who will find themselves shut out and deprived.

Admittance into the Kingdom of God, at the present time within you only, but later, when the Lord of Hosts comes, on earth as in heaven, is such a precious important matter for your true selves that it is worth sacrificing everything to obtain.[55-56] Such admittance can only be by the gate, the one true path of faith, obedience and service[57-58] and by strict adherence to my teachings, not to those of persons acting on my behalf for money.[59] Meanwhile, be most vigilant against deception, especially by those who pretend to be of your membership and in authority; you can test them for they cause disharmony, strife, discord, divisions, and do not adhere to my teachings.[60] If you succeed in maintaining vigilance over yourselves, watching that your hearts are not seduced by worldly enticements, you will indeed be rewarded and happy when your Lord comes.[61] You would do well then to attain to the greatest greatest degree of humility, for that is especially rewarded.[62]

The coming of the Kingdom of God means that God will come to claim His own for Himself, for a permanent possession, to rule over the hearts of men, but you do not know when it comes as it will come without your knowing it[63] at an unexpected time,[64] so you must watch and be prepared. You will know it by the fact that people will appear who demonstrate the true life of the spirit and the ancient faith of God will be renewed.[65] If Judaism at that time, despite the coming of the successive messengers of God, does not respond, then it will be wholly brought to an end.[66] Even a worldly authority reacts eventually to continual importuning and exacts justice; so will God, if He finds His people are sore oppressed, take a just vengeance.[67] Nevertheless, in spite of everything, any person, indeed even mankind as a whole, though lured away from the path of loving dutiful obedience by seductive worldly enticement of lower nature and grosser appetites, after spending all his energies and powers upon them, will be warmly welcomed back to the Kingdom of God if sincerely penitent and desiring to change his ways.[68] When the earth in its pregnancy casts its burden and the Kingdom of God is brought forth there will indeed be rejoicing.[69]

Such, or something like it, seems to be the general purport of the parables of Jesus, both those which relate to the renewal of faith and religion which He came to effect, and those in which He referred to the impending emergence of the Kingdom of God, a phenomenon related to the natural law, the will of God, yet due to be inaugurated by His own return in the glory of the Father, the Lord of Hosts, and on its inauguration, at an unknown time, to come unexpectedly upon mankind with membership assured for the vigilant faithful and denied to the negligent, the indifferent, the insincere, the ungodly, the oppressors, the priesthoods (husbandmen, hirelings, false prophets in sheep's clothing).

Chapter 9

MIRACLES

A major feature of the ministry of Jesus, as recorded in the Gospels, are the miracles He performed, and no discussion of the Christianity of Jesus would be complete without some consideration of the miracles.

All the Founders of the great world religions performed miracles, in the sense that They enacted deeds beyond the capacity of other people which are inexplicable except in terms of the possession of supra-normal powers. Just as miracles are related of Krishna, of Buddha, of Zoroaster, so too we know of the miraculous actions of Moses in regard to the plagues of Egypt, water from a rock, dividing the Red Sea, manna from heaven, etc. and we know of Muhammad Whose Quran is a supreme miracle for an illiterate man. Miracles are reported of several other great men in the Old Testament, for example of Elijah challenging the priests of Baal when he called down fire from heaven. Miracles are recorded as performed by some of the apostles after the passing of Jesus Himself. Remarkable events, amounting to miracles, are reported of many modern doctors, of faith healers. Many private individuals have reported events that for them are miraculous, or beyond explanation by known factors of causation.

Miracles are therefore universal, if relatively rare, phenomena. They are also effective as persuaders of truth only for those who witness them or experience them, and not always then. A small core of scepticism is always liable to lie in the breasts of those who receive account of miracles at second hand. When He healed a man from leprosy He expressly said "See thou say nothing to any man"[1]

Another obvious point needs also to be made. If miracles are regarded as being proof of supra-normal powers because of their physical effects, then they are of small value indeed. A person raised from physical death to physical life will die again, and a person receiving back physical sight or physical hearing will lose it again when physical death finally occurs. Whatever then may be the physical effects they are far less than the value of the miracles if they can be regarded as spiritual deeds expressed symbolically in physical terms. To renew the faith of someone who has lapsed is an eternal bounty and a far greater deed, perhaps a far more difficult deed, then the merely temporary amelioration of a physical condition of abnormality.

When we read what Jesus Himself said about miracles we can see that He surely thought along these lines and intended His followers to do likewise.

On several notable occasions He specifically rejected the use of His special powers and of miracles to prove His mission.

During His withdrawal for the vigil in the wilderness at the outset of His ministry He disclaimed in very vigorous terms the idea that He should use His special powers either for Himself or to persuade others in a way they could not help but acknowledge. Man's life does not depend on the physical alone but needs the Word of God for its sustenance and enlargement.[2] Faith requires to be tested so as to grow, and unbelief bludgeoned into belief is not necessarily altered in attitude, behaviour or deeds.

Even more specifically Jesus twice said, [3] " An evil and adulterous generation seeketh after a sign; and there shall no sign be given to it, but the sign of the prophet Jonas." The real miracle of Christianity, in other words, is the establishment of the Cause of Jesus by His God-intoxicated disciples, so few in number, after the apparent extinction of that Cause for three days, through the emergence into vital, living presence of His reality in their inner selves after they had been thrown into despair and confusion by His Crucifixion.

Again, and in a remarkable passage, Jesus says, " For judgment I am come unto this world, that they which see not might see; and they which see might be made blind."[4] There is no record of Jesus causing anyone to go blind physically, so that this must clearly be taken as having a spiritual or inner meaning. If this half of the passage has an inner meaning, surely it is legitimate to suppose that restoring sight or granting sight should also be interpreted spiritually.

There are 70 miracles recorded in the four Gospels counting separately when a miracle seems to be recorded more than once but counting as one the several apperances after the crucifixion; 22 in Matthew, 19 in Mark, 21 in Luke and 8 in John. A full list of them is set out in Appendix E.

Many of these miracles can be taken at face value, so to speak, as they have been taken for centuries, and when so taken are often vivid illustrations of the compassion of Jesus for the unfortunate, e.g. the cleansing of lepers, the restoration of sight or speech or hearing, the casting out of devils, the healing of an ear of the high priest's servant, even the feeding of a hungry multitude.

All the miracles however take on deeper significance, a fresh dimension of value, when examined for inner or spiritual meaning. As such they can be grouped thus:

1. Those which relate to the life of the spirit, renewal of faith in God, the effecting of a change of heart, mind, attitude, behaviour. To this group belong all the healing miracles where Jesus

cures people of waywardness, perversity, fanaticism, paralysis of will, misdirection of energy, etc.

2. Those which relate to the illumination of the understanding, the opening of the inner eye of spiritual insight. To this group belong the transfiguration and the appearances after the crucifixion.

3. Those which illustrate the powers of the spirit, like a parable expressed as a miracle. To this group belong the feeding of the spiritually starved masses, the calming of the storm of human strife and confusion, the walking above the sea of materialism, the cursing of the figtree.

4. Those demonstrating faith in action, reliance on the Word of God. To this group belong the discovery of the piece of money for tribute in the fish's mouth, the large catch of fish.

5. That demonstating the revitalising effect of the new message, notably the turning water into wine at the marriage feast of Cana.

Often enough the Gospel commentary, as distinct from the actual words and deeds of Jesus, makes reference to a more literal interpretation of these miracles.[5] The intention of this exposition is not to deny that a physical interpretation of the miracles is possible, or that physical effects were not apparent. Rather it is hoped to suggest that another interpretation is not only possible but desirable and more valuable far for understanding and appreciation of the mission of Jesus and His Christianity.

Apart from the points already mentioned regarding the temptations, the refusal to give a sign, the making of people blind, there are also other indications that the spiritual view is a right one. Forgiveness of sins,[6] divisions and blasphemies [7] are associated with healing in a number of places, and Jesus clearly indicates that people at that time for the most part are not intended to have a deeper understanding of His words and actions " lest at any time they should see with their eyes, and hear with their ears, and should understand with their hearts and should be converted, and I should heal them ",[8] and this where there is no hint of physical disability or illness.

It is also worthy of mention that there were occasions when Jesus did not perform a healing miracle when He might have done, for when one of the disciples asked Him to let him go and bury his father before obeying His call, Jesus said, " Follow me; and let the dead bury their dead ",[9] clearly referring to those dead in the spirit burying those who were physically dead. " That which is born of the flesh is flesh; and that which is born of the Spirit is spirit."[10]

Chapter 10

A COHERENT PATTERN

Several different ways suggest themselves to building up a coherent picture or pattern of the ministry and teachings of the Lord Christ. Two such will be attempted:

i pattern derived from assembling together the positive and negative injunctions, precepts, attributes and actions.

ii pattern based on the sixfold purpose of the ministry, to fulfil, to confirm, to abrogate, to judge, to institute, to herald, which we derived from the analysis of purposes stated by Himself (see above page 68).

In each case the actual words of Jesus will be examined so far as possible rather than what tradition has handed down regarding the setting of His ministry of the recorded results of the expository statements of early followers.

1 *Pattern derived from His teachings and deeds, positive and negative*

Christ's positive precepts and injunctions were very numerous and were expressed in several different ways, to individuals singly or in small or large groups, by direct imperative, by emphatic assertion, by parable, by oblique statement, by personal action, by demeanour, and they were delivered both in private to His closest associates and in public before larger numbers of common people, of specialists, of officials both secular and religious.

The different gospels, because of their different authors, their different purposes, their different dates, present somewhat different patterns as one would expect. It is as though four different facets of a large and flawless diamond had been presented for view, three of them, close together and of similar shape and cut, reflecting slightly different but nonetheless similar lights from a point just within the surface, while the fourth is at a quite different angle, compensating for its relatively smaller size or surface area by the purer and more brilliant light from a greater depth within the stone. John's gospel is surely profounder and more luminous though with fewer ' lights ' and less detail than any of the others.

What pattern are we to infer from the precepts and injunctions of Christ as recorded in the Gospels of Mark and John?

75

Let us look again at the injunctions, especially those in Mark's Gospel—*i*, to individuals; *ii*, to His enemies; *iii*, to His disciples; *iv*, to mankind at large:

1. To individuals Christ was uncompromising: the divisive influences were to come out and be silent, the individuals themselves to act with positive resoluteness—' arise ', ' stand forth ', ' stretch out ', ' go thy way ', ' go in peace ', ' be whole ', ' be clean ', ' be unafraid ', ' believe '.

What qualities are these but initiative, action, peacefulness, wholesomeness, cleanliness, courage, faith, and steadily living one's own life?

II. Towards the scribes and Pharisees, the theologians and divines of the age, Christ adopted a clear irrefutable line. With one or two, who were sincere, He responded with some of the greatest of His statements, with Nicodemus, a Pharisee, for example (1) indicating the reality of spiritual conversion and clarifying His own station and mission, and with one of the scribes, (2) with the glorious summary of religion itself as an attitude of love towards God expressed through life with other people. Towards others, however, He responded with vigour. Where unity has a divine foundation it is not for man to create disunity, specifically about marriage, and generally surely also about God's order established on earth, the society brought into being by the believers. He calls for recognition of divine authority as the basis for religious action and enjoins obedience to authority, whether of God or of Caesar, making no distinction between the attitude and attribute to be shown.

The qualities enjoined are: unity, recognition of authority, obedience.

III. To His disciples Christ gave much fuller indication of His precepts, but because they were people of no great standing and mostly of poor education, who had been attracted to His call to follow Him, not at first understanding the reasons for His influence over them, He treated them gently, leading them gradually forward to deeper understanding of His own real self and the purpose of His ministry. Christ's injunctions to His disciples tend to get more important and more intimate as His ministry draws to a close.

What then were the disciples to do?

They were to:

1. Follow Him and His example.
2. Teach His gospel or glad tidings.
3. Attract the hearts of individuals.
4. Do the will of God and so become spiritually related to Him.
5. Shun gossip and backbiting.
6. Feed the Word of God (the bread of Christ's perfections), to the hungry, spiritually famished multitudes.

7. Know He was with them in every crisis which He had demonstrable power to surmount.
8. Be audacious.
9. Beware the influences and contagion of worldly, ambitious and intellectual people.
10. Beware especially their own personal tempters.
11. Encourage whoever does good even though not of their own membership.
12. Eliminate ruthlessly any of their own members, however eminent, who obstruct them in their work.
13. Maintain the closest unity, solidarity and mutuality among themselves.
14. Teach the children and take on their qualities of open candour, sincerity, innocence.
15. Be confident that God was with them in all they did.
16. Know that prayer will be answered.
17. Overlook faults and harbour no antagonism towards anyone, at moment of prayer.
18. Watch out for deceit.
19. Be untroubled by future crises and conflicts however severe.
20. Watch their own weaknesses.
21. Know that if brought to trial and test they would be fortified and aided in response by the Holy Spirit.
22. Be ready to flee unencumbered to the mountains when Daniel's prophecy was fulfilled.
23. Disbelieve those who claimed to expound Christ in various ways.
24. Recognise new life in the tree of divine religion when it renewed itself.
25. Be vigilant, heedful, prayerful, as they could not know when the time would come.
26. Allow personal extravagance in His path, when shown from the fulness of the heart.
27. Prepare the upper chamber of their minds and spirits for His special remembrance and the celebration of the last supper.
28. Take hold of and absorb to themselves (take, eat) His real spiritual bounties and perfections (His body: the bread of life).
29. Be wakeful and full of prayer against tests.
30. Be alert for His return.
31. Go out and tell the world the glad tidings.

Who else up to that time had ever given such explicit teaching for His followers? These 30 or so precepts surely convey a clear picture of His expectations for those who really believed in Him.

IV.   With mankind at large Christ was naturally less specific, more general in His injunctions, but He clearly expected a great

77

deal, whether or not those who listened were His own followers. These precepts are few, but they seem to anticipate a considerable measure of acceptance of His authority, if not of His religion. They contain their proportion of warnings, as do the precepts addressed to other groups or individuals.

He expected mankind to:

1. Turn back to obedience and belief in God and His message.
2. Listen and
3. get to know His words.
4. Practise self-mastery
5. Accept one's individual place in life.
6. Emulate His example if they would be His followers.
7. Acknowledge the passing of the former dispensation of Moses.
8. Look out for intellectual leaders who put on special garments, seek to be accorded public honour, expect special treatment in religious assembly and at social gatherings, obtain their living by taking advantage of the unprotected, use long prayers like parrots or without sincerity.
9. Be specially heedful and alert against the day of His own return.

Another way of deriving a clear understanding of Christ's message is to put His precepts and injunctions negatively, indicating what He expected His followers not to do:

If we take the 30 or more injunctions to His disciples in Mark's Gospel which we have just reviewed positively, and put them negatively, we find that Christ expected them not to:

1. Turn their backs on Him.
2. Keep to themselves their knowledge of His gospel.
3. Ignore those they met who might respond to the message.
4. Follow their own selfish, petty pursuits.
5. Open themselves to gossip and backbiting.
6. Shun the crying need of the masses for guidance and help.
7. Forget His availability and presence at all times.
8. Be timid and withdrawing.
9. Allow the infection of the worldly wise, the ambitious, the intellectually proud, to take control.
10. Let their own Satan be their guide.
11. Suppress the well-doer because he is not of the orthodox.
12. Continue meekly with the cancer of obstructionists within their own ranks.
13. Drift towards a savourless disharmony.
14. Take no thought of the children, their upbringing or the special qualities they bring to society when rightly nurtured.
15. Be heedless of and distrust God.
16. Doubt the efficacy of prayer.

17. Harbour ill-will towards anyone.
18. Permit infiltration by the unscrupulous.
19. Be deeply concerned and worry over worldly strife and crises.
20. Become complacent about their own weaknesses.
21. Make excuses or plan ahead calculatingly if challenged or tested.
22. Stay at home ' with head under the pillow ' when Daniel's prophecy takes effect.
23. Turn to listen to every exponent who claims authority.
24. Suppose that no renewal of divine truth will ever take place.
25. Forget heedlessly the coming of the time of the end.
26. Condemn personal sacrifice and extravagance without taking account of the motive.
27. Permit His remembrance and the last supper to become perfunctory or a matter of mere conformity.
28. Turn His remembrance into a superstition or disregard it altogether.
29. " Fall asleep " and be unconscious of the danger of temptation.
20. Neglect His promised return.
31. Stay at home and keep to themselves His glorious message.

(It is realised that several of these would be expressed rather differently by others, and that some of them are not easy to put in the opposite sense, notably nos. 18, 20, 21, 22 and 28.)

An important point that needs to be acknowledged when considering these injunctions, when expressed in the negative sense, is that wherever any one of them is practised by an individual or a group of people, anti-Christ rules instead of Christ. A conclusion that might be reached is that whereas there undoubtedly are many individuals who are sincerely endeavouring to live a life that matches these precepts and injunctions, the preponderant majority is doing otherwise and no nation or government in the world today, however much it may suppose that its laws and customs are based upon Christianity, is really making the slightest attempt to carry these precepts into effect, even those which they could regard as appropriate, eg. nos, 4, 6, 9, 13, 14, 15, 16, 17, 18, 19, 20.

The Sermon on the Mount

One of the best known parts of the Gospels is the Sermon on the Mount. Let us examine it in the same way and see what it yields by way of definite injunctions, qualities inculcated and, by inference, negatives to be avoided.

The Sermon on the Mount comprises three chapters (5 to 7) of Matthew's Gospel. The imperatives are many, 56 of them in all (some linked together in context), and as imperatives from the holiest Source are surely more vital and necessary to attempt performance

than the more famous precepts, 9 in number, which are but per-
missive in form (" Blessed are the poor in spirit, the mourners, the
meek, those hungry for righteousness, the merciful, the pure in
heart, the peacemakers, those persecuted for rightousness' sake,
those subjected to calumny for My sake "). Obedience to the clear
imperatives is necessary and prerequisite: to act in the way that
attracts one of the stipulated rewards is desirable and carries the
added reward of happiness and bountiful blessing.

What are these imperatives?

" Rejoice, and be exceeding glad " (5: 12).

" Let your light so shine before men . . ." (5: 6).

" Think not that I am come to destroy the law . . . (5: 17).

" Leave there thy gift before the altar, and go thy way: first be
reconciled to thy brother, and then come and offer thy
gift .. (5: 24).

" Agree with thine adversary quickly, whilst thou art in the
way with him . . ." 5: 25).

" And if thy right eye offend thee, pluck it out, and cast it
from thee . . . and if thy right hand offend thee, cut it off,
and cast it from thee . . ." (5:29-30).

" Swear not at all . . . but let your communication be, Yea,
Yea; Nay, nay . . ." (5: 33-37).

" . . . that ye resist not evil: but whosoever shall smite thee
on thy right cheek, turn to him the other also " (5: 39).

" And if any man will sue thee at the law, and take away thy
coat, let him have thy cloak also " (5: 40).

" And whosoever shall compel thee to go a mile, go with him
twain " (5: 41).

" Give to him that asketh thee, and from him that would
borrow of thee turn not thou away " (5: 42).

" Love your enemies, bless them that curse you, do good to
them that hate you, and pray for them which despitefully use
you and persecute you " (5: 44).

" Be ye therefore perfect, even as your Father which is in
heaven is perfect " (5: 48).

" Take heed that ye do not your alms before men, to be seen
of them . . . therefore when thou doest thine alms do not
sound a trumpet before thee . . . but when thou doest
alms, let not thy left hand know what thy right hand doeth "
6: 1-3).

" But thou, when thou prayest, enter into thy closet, and when
thou hast shut the door, pray to thy Father which is in
secret . . . but when ye pray, use not vain repetitions, as
the heathen do . . . be ye not therefore like unto them . . .
After this manner therefore pray ye . . ." (6: 6-9).

" Moreover when ye fast, be not as the hypocrites, of a sad
countenance . . . but thou, when thou fastest, anoint thy
head and wash thy face " (6:16-17).

" Lay not up for yourselves treasures upon earth . . . but lay up for yourselves treasure in heaven " (6: 19-20).

" Take no thought for your life, what ye shall eat, or what ye shall drink; nor yet for your body, what ye shall put on . . . Behold the fowls of the air . . . Consider the lilies of the field, how they grow . . . therefore take no thought, saying, ' What shall we eat?' or ' What shall we drink?' or, ' Wherewithal shall we be clothed?' . . . But seek ye first the kingdom of God, and his righteousness . . . Take therefore no thought for tomorrow " (6: 25-34).

" Judge not, that ye be not judged " (7: 1).

" Thou hypocrite, first cast out the beam out of thine own eye " (7: 5).

" Give not that which is holy unto the dogs, neither cast ye pearls before swine " (7: 6).

" Ask, and it shall be given you; seek, and ye shall find; knock, and it shall be opened unto you " (7: 7).

" All things whatsoever ye would that men should do to you, do ye even so to them; for this is the law and the prophets " (7: 12).

" Enter ye in at the strait gate " (7: 13).

" Beware of false prophets, which come to you in sheep's clothing " (7: 15).

By rephrasing these we can perhaps get nearer to the qualities and attributes that are to be developed through the actions resulting from obedience to these imperatives:

' Be radiant and joyful with the light of the spirit of faith and service—always present the positive aspects of My fulfilling message (I may change the external social rules and ordinances, but I deepen the spirit of faith and fulfil promises made)—never perpetuate a source of contention, expecially when engaged in service to the work of God: unity and harmony within your ranks comes before your work for Me—do not let disagreements fester, work them out to a harmonious conclusion as quickly as you can—no matter how valuable and respected a member within your ranks, if he obstructs you, have no more to do with him—do not use imprecations or oaths, but simple statements: control your temper—in your dealings with an individual, one to one, always give way allowing him twice what he seeks and giving or lending when he asks, or demands or compels: you attract beauty of character to yourself that way and he perhaps learns from you—be like the sun and radiate love, bounty, good and prayers on all, even on those who curse, hate and illtreat you: you must be radiant all through and in all circumstances—seek to acquire perfections and to make progress always.'

' Give to charity, but do it privately—pray in private with sincere hearts using the prayer I give you—observe the fast for the sake of God, preparing yourself in advance, and with happy spirit— do not seek to be distinguished for your worldly possessions or achievements, but for your qualities of spirit, for those intangible eternal rewards of right action—put first always and focus on the work of establishing God's kingdom and your problems will be solved, for He will supply your needs as He provides for the birds and the flowers.'

' Do not look for faults in others and criticise them, rather take steps to remove the negative tendency in yourself which leads you to find fault—preserve and keep safe the precious holy message and do not offer it to the selfish and ungodly—persevere in your quest always and you will surely attain—do to others as you would have them do to you—keep on towards the gateway of life—look out especially for those who pretend to be of your own ranks of the faithful (" in sheep's clothing ") but are really self-seeking creatures of perdition leading you astray '.

What then are the qualities He calls for from those who listen and obey? Surely they are these : Radiant joyfulness of spirit—active teaching of His fulfilling message—unity and harmony together—avoidance of dispute—self-control and calm conversation—generous acquiescence towards any individual—bountiful, prayerful love towards enemies as persons—struggle towards progress to betterment—avoidance of ostentation in giving—sincerity in prayer—observance of fasting for the sake of God—seeking spiritual rather than worldly distinction—focussing on work for God's kingdom—appreciation of others, not fault-finding—protection of the holy message from alien, ungodly contact—perseverance towards goals with confidence of achievement—genuine mutuality and reciprocity with others—special watchfulness against deceivers within the ranks of the army of God.

It will be recalled that when Jesus was on the cross, the four soldiers on guard took His clothes and shared them out among themselves but found His coat to be seamless, so they cast lots to decide who should have it.[3] We have now scanned carefully both the Gospel of John and the Gospel of Mark and have reached the firm conclusion that, like that seamless coat, the Cause, the teachings, the foundation of the Christianity of Jesus Christ was in one piece at its beginning, that His commandments, precepts, warnings, personal example and life were both internally self-consistent, all luminously radiant, vibrant with life-giving spirit, as manifestations of the glorious Sun of Truth, and all wholly consistent with reason, with logic, and with science.

The second way we proposed to follow for showing a coherent pattern in the ministry and teachings of the Lord Christ, was to outline the sixfold purpose of His mission—to fulfil, to confirm, to abrogate, to judge, to institute, to herald. (cf. P. 68).

Fulfilment of the Old Testament

Jesus was a Jew born of Mary who married into the royal line of David, was scrupulous in His observance of most Jewish practice and was careful to give good precedent wherever He departed from that practice. From the early years of His visit with His family to Jerusalem, He was to go often to the Holy City, for the celebration of the Passover and the Feast of Tabernacles. He took vigorous and symbolic action to cleanse the Temple of commercial traffickers and He wept over the fate of the City itself which He foresaw was destined for total destruction.

Jesus was at pains to relate His ministry to the expectations of the Old Testament, the Pentateuch of Moses and the books of the lesser prophets. He read from the scriptures in the synagogues in the early stage of His ministry and expounded the passages He read in a way that challenged the orthodox and caused a fierce reaction.[4] When he occasionally abrogated or modified the existing law He took great care to justify His action.[5]

Through His mother He was descended from Abraham, by Sarah. In passing it may be remarked that Jesus' permanent place in all history may in some degree derive from the fact that He stands a little apart, that He brought no code of law, that His teachings were of pure spirit, therefore eternal. Unlike other Messengers of God descended from Abraham, He will forever share the realm of human hearts with the Father, between Whom and Himself there can be no distinction made save that of the comprehensiveness of truth revealed to man. Forever will Christ's teachings move the heart and spiritualise the soul of the individual, complementing the mighty work of the Father come to quicken and unite the whole human family.

Jesus made frequent use in quotation and verbal allusion of the Old Testament (Old Covenant), but specific fulfilment of Old Testament promises by Him included the following:

1. " And Moses took the blood, and sprinkled it on the people, and said, Behold the blood of the covenant, which the Lord hath made with you concerning all these words."[6]
2. " Ye shall not tempt the Lord your God . . ."[7]
3. " Let not them that are mine enemies wrongfully rejoice over me: neither let them wink with the eye that hate me without a cause." (Psalm 35: 19) and " They that hate me without a cause are more than the hairs of mine head: they that would destroy me, being mine enemies wrongfully, are mighty: then I restored that which I took not away."[8]
4. " Yea mine own familiar friend, in whom I trusted, which did eat of my bread, hath lifted up his heel against me."[9]
5. " And had rained down manna upon them to eat, and had given them of the corn of heaven."[10]
6. " When he shall be judged, let him be condemned: and let his prayer become sin. Let his days be few; and let another take his office."[11]

7. " The Lord said unto my Lord, Sit thou at my right hand, until I make thine enemies thy footstool."[12]

8. " The stone which the builders refused is become the head stone of the corner."[13]

9. " And he said, Go, and tell this people, Hear ye indeed, but understand not; and see ye indeed, but perceive not. Make the heart of this people fat, and make their ears heavy, and shut their eyes; lest they see with their eyes, and hear with their ears, and understand with their heart, and convert, and be healed."[14]

10. " Wherefore the Lord said, Forasmuch as this people draw near me with their mouth, and with their lips do honour me, but have removed their heart far from me, and fear toward me is taught by the precept of men."[15]

11. " Then the eyes of the blind shall be opened, and the ears of the deaf shall be unstopped."[16]

12. " And all thy children shall be taught of the Lord; and great shall be the peace of thy children."[17]

13. " Therefore will I divide him a portion with the great, and he shall divide the spoil with the strong; because he hath poured out his soul unto death: and he was numbered with the transgressors; and he bare the sin of many, and made intercession for the transgressors."[18]

14. " The spirit of the Lord God is upon me; because the Lord hath anointed me to preach good tidings unto the meek; he hath sent me to bind up the broken-hearted, to proclaim liberty to the captives, and the opening of the prison to them that are bound; to proclaim the acceptable year of the Lord, and the day of vengeance of our God; to comfort all that mourn."[19]

15. " And he shall confirm the covenant with many for one week: and in the midst of the week he shall cause the sacrifice and the oblation to cease, and for the over-spreading of abominations he shall make it desolate, even until the consummation, and that determined shall be poured upon the desolate." (Daniel 9:27). " And from the time that the daily sacrifice shall be taken away, and the abomination that maketh desolate set up, there shall be a thousand two hundred and ninety days."[20]

16. For the son dishonoureth the father, the daughter riseth up against her mother, the daughter in law against her mother in law; a man's enemies are the men of his own house."[21]

17. " Awake, O sword, against my shepherd, and against the man that is my fellow, saith the Lord of hosts: smite the shepherd, and the sheep shall be scattered: and I will turn mine hand upon the little ones."[22]

18. " Behold, I will send my messenger, and he will prepare the way before me: and the Lord, whom ye seek, shall suddenly come to his temple, even the messenger of the covenant, whom ye delight in: behold, he shall come, saith the Lord of hosts."[23]

19. " Behold, I will send you Elijah the prophet before the coming of the great and dreadful day of the Lord: and he shall turn the heart of the fathers to the children, and the heart of the children to their fathers, lest I come and smite the earth with a curse."[24]

In the case of these 19 quotations it is Christ Himself Who indicates the relationship of fulfilment directly or obliquely. In about another 30 passages the writers of the Gospels make direct reference to specific places in the Old Testament.

It is worth remarking that neither Christ nor these writers of the Gospels laid claim to fulfil the famous passages in Isaiah of which so much has been made by later generations of Christians, in chapters 9 and 11—" For unto us a child is born . . ." and " And there shall come forth a rod out of the stem of Jesse . . ." Fulfilment has been claimed for Him by enthusiastic followers who overlooked the clear indications left by Christ that He did not fulfil them. For Jesus said, " My kingdom is not of this world "[25] " I am come not to send peace, but a sword ",[26] and although He identified Himself with the Father in the passage " I and the Father are one ",[27] He also affirmed that the Father had knowledge of which he was deprived,[28] and He had authority not possessed by Himself.[29] In making this disavowal Christ also made clear that the Spirit of Truth would come to lead to all truth.[30]

Relationship to Moses

Many people forget the extent and depth of recognition accorded to Moses in the Gospels. There are at least 26 references to Moses, Jesus Himself mentioning him 14 times, many more than any other personage of the Old Testament, indeed more often than all other Old Testament personages put together. In perhaps the most significant of those passages,[31] Jesus clearly implied that the written words of Moses were as worthy of credence, belief, faith as His own spoken words: both carried the same authority. " If ye believe (have faith in) not his writings, how shall ye believe my words?"

Jesus reminded His hearers of the validity of the ordinances of Moses but clearly indicated also that He was empowered to vary them.[32] He maintained that the scribes and Pharisees had usurped and abused the authority of Moses, " for they say, and do not ",[33] that Moses taught immortality[34] so clearly that if they had faith in Him as a true intermediary with God that would be sufficient and far more effective than if someone rose from the dead: indeed such an event in itself would not prove sufficient ground for belief. Moses gave the Jews bread from heaven in the form of manna for

85

their physical sustenance, Jesus brought spiritual life-giving bread, his teachings and perfections given Him by His Father, to share with His followers.[35] Jesus expressly fulfilled prophecies " written in the law of Moses " concerning him.[36]

In one other passage[37] Jesus linked Himself with Moses in a way that deserves close attention. Moses was commanded to make " a fiery serpent and set it upon a pole so that everyone who is bitten when he looketh upon it, shall live ".[38] Again there is a contrast drawn between the physical effects of the particular action of Moses, and the spiritual life-giving effect upon the believers in Jesus when they looked upon Him " set upon a pole " in crucifixion. " As Moses lifted up the serpent in the wilderness, even so must the Son of man be lifted up ". There is much more than that to the significance of the passage as can be seen if we study the verses before and after. Jesus was speaking to Nicodemus of the necessity to be born again of the spirit, to be converted, to generate the spirit of faith. The people of Israel had sinned so the Lord had sent a plague of " fiery serpents " among them as a punishment; when they repented they were required to have faith in the efficacy of the brass serpent which Moses was ordered to set upon a pole so that if they looked at it they would be healed. Jesus, as He was standing there with Nicodemus, said, " No man hath ascended up to heaven, but he that came down from heaven, even the Son of man which is in heaven ". Thus " heaven " is clearly a condition or state which Jesus possessed or occupied while walking and talking. It was a condition or state which others might attain when He had been set upon a pole and the spirit of life-giving faith was engendered in those who turned to Him; they would have the eternal spiritual life of heaven, the second birth of the spirit. First the response, then the belief, then the action based on that belief, then the reward of eternal life—a qualitative heavenly condition of the spirit or soul.

" Had ye believed Moses, ye would have believed me, for he wrote of me " (Jn. 5: 46).

The Ten Commandments

The great commandments of God given through Moses were confirmed explicitly by Jesus[39], but He also gave each of them added point and deeper spiritual meaning, enriched them with new dimensions.

    1. " I am the Lord thy God, which have brought thee out of the land of Egypt, out of the house of bondage. Thou shalt have no other gods before me ".[40]

        Jesus confirmed this commandment when He said, " The first of all the commandments is ' Hear, O Israel, the Lord our God is one Lord '"[41] but He greatly strengthened it and deepened it when He added, " And thou shalt love the Lord thy God with all they heart, and with all thy soul, and with all thy mind, and with all thy strength "[42]

2. " Thou shalt not make unto thee any graven image, or any likeness of anything that is in the heavens above, or that is in the earth beneath, or that is in the waters under the earth: thou shalt not bow down thyself to them, nor serve them: for I the Lord thy God am a jealous God, visiting the iniquities of the fathers upon the children unto the third and fourth generation of them that hate me; and showing mercy unto thousands of them that love me and keep my commandments ".[43]

Jesus enhanced and enriched this commandment when He said, " God is a spirit: and they that worship Him must worship Him in spirit and in truth ".[44]

3. " Thou shalt not take the name of the Lord thy God in vain; for the Lord will not hold him guiltless that taketh his name in vain ".[45]

Jesus was more emphatic still when he said, " Swear not at all . . . but let your communication be ' Yea, yea; Nay, nay; for whatsoever is more than these cometh of evil ".[46] God's name was holy and a man's bare word should be sufficient for total reliability.

4. " Remember the Sabbath day to keep it holy . . .".[47]

Moses thus set apart the seventh day to be reserved and kept holy. Jesus, however, making clear that He was " Lord also of the Sabbath ",[48] taught that all time was God's to do good in. God was present everywhere and always, so long as He was worshipped in spirit and in truth, and wherever two or three came together in His name He was present among them,[49] not just on a special day only. Early Christians did not set apart one special day for worship as holier than others.

5. " Honour thy father and thy mother: that thy days may be long upon the land which the Lord thy God giveth thee ".[50]

Jesus reiterated this commandment along with the others,[51] but made certain modifications. His first recorded act was to leave Joseph and Mary that He might go to the Temple and " be about my Father's business ".[52] He indicated that He had " come to set a man at variance against his father, and the daughter against her mother ".[53] The priorities are clear anough: first the business of God or His Messenger, then honour and respect to parents until the time of marriage,[54] but honour to parents except when it clashes with the overriding higher duty to God[52] must be maintained and most certainly it must not be by-passed by mere technicalities.[55]

6. "Thou shalt not kill".[56]

Jesus said to Peter, "Put up again thy sword into its place"[57] and " all they that take the sword shall perish with the sword".[58] He stated, "Blessed are the peacemakers: for they shall be called the children of God"[59] clearly indicating that warmongers are the opposite. He emphasised that He had come that His people might "have life and have it more abundantly".[60] He called on people to love their enemies, to forgive, to do good, to be generous, to be merciful, and forbade them to criticize and condemn.[61]

7. "Thou shalt not commit adultery".[62]

Jesus went much further when He said, "Whosoever looketh on a woman to lust after her hath committed adultery with her already in his heart".[63]

8. "Thou shalt not steal".[64]

Jesus, after reiterating this among the other great commandments, went onto counsel laying up treasure in heaven through selling up and giving to the poor.[65] Even if this counsel be regarded as specific to the particular individual He addressed, Jesus said elsewhere that His followers must lay up treasure in heaven[66] for where their treasure was there also would their heart be.[67] He also enjoined them to aim at perfection.[68]

9. "Thou shalt not bear false witness against thy neighbour".[69]

The views expressed by Jesus about hypocrisy are sufficiently numerous and emphatic for it to be inferred that He utterly condemned lying in any form. He even elevated the true attitude to a neighbour to the position of the second of the two greatest commandments, "Thou shalt love thy neighbour as thyself".[70]

10. "Thou shalt not covet . . .".[71]

Often Jesus enjoined that His followers should be ready to part with their goods for the benefit of others, of those in need. He indicated too, for example in the parable of the good Samaritan, that anyone at all is one's neighbour, not merely those who live nearby or are of the same race, religion or social status.

Confirmation of Moses

No more certain fact emerges from reading the Gospels than the realisation of the total conjunction of purpose, authority and viewpoint between Jesus and Moses. Some 1400 years had passed since the mission of Moses had been triumphantly concluded with the children of Israel re-educated, moulded into a people with a new way of life, about to take possession of the promised land to which He had led them through such difficulties and dangers for so long a time, Yet, the teachings, the ordinances and the commandments of Moses are unhesitatingly quoted by Jesus as wholly authoritative on all suitable situations. Indeed Jesus saw fit to make very few explicit changes, as will be seen later.

Jesus makes more specific references to Moses, the High Prophet of the Jews, than to all the other prophets put together. These specific references are instructive:

1. " See thou say nothing to any man: but go thy way, show thyself to the priest, and offer for thy cleansing those things which Moses commanded, for a testimony unto them ".[72]This He said to a man He had ' healed ' of leprosy and the reference is to requirements set forth in Leviticus[73] and Deuteronomy.[74]

2. Jesus challenging the hypocrisy of the Pharisees, says: " Moses said ' Honour thy father and thy mother ' and ' Whoso curseth father or mother, let him die the death ' ".[75]

3. " What did Moses command you? (about divorce) and they (the Pharisees) said, Moses suffered to write a bill of divorcement, and to put her away. And Jesus answered, and said unto them, ' For the hardness of your hearts he wrote you this precept ' ".[76]

4. " Thou knowest the commandments, Do not commit adultery, Do not kill, Do not steal, Do not bear false witness, Defraud not, Honour thy father and mother ". So Jesus to the rich young man asking of eternal life.[77]

5. " And as touching the dead that they rise, have ye not read in the book of Moses, how in the bush God spake unto him, saying, ' I am the God of Abraham, and the God of Isaac, and the God of Jacob?' ".[78]

6. Jesus in answer to one of the scribes who expressed appreciation of His replies, " The first of all the commandments is, ' Hear, O Israel: the Lord our God is one Lord: and thou shalt love the Lord thy God with all thy heart, and with all thy soul, and with all thy mind, and with all thy strength!: this is the first commandment and the second is like, namely this, ' Thou shalt love thy neighbour as thyself ' ".[79]

7. Under temptation in the wilderness Jesus said, " It is written, ' Man shall not live by bread alone, but by every word that proceedeth out of the mouth of God ' ".[80]

8. Also in the wilderness, " It is written again, ' Thou shalt not tempt the Lord thy God ' ".[81]

9. Also in the wilderness, " It is written ' Thou shalt worship the Lord thy God, and him only shalt thou serve ' ".[82]

10. In the Sermon on the Mount, " Ye have heard that it was said by them of old time, Thou shalt not kill; and whosoever shall kill shall be in danger of the judgment ".[83]

11. Also in the Sermon on the Mount—" ye have heard that it was said by them of old time, Thou shalt not commit adultery ".[84]
12. Also in the Sermon on the Mount—" Again, ye have heard that it hath been said by them of old time, Thou shalt not forswear thyself, but shalt perform unto the Lord thine oaths ".[85]
13. Also in the Sermon on the Mount—" Ye have heard that it hath been said, An eye for an eye, and a tooth for a tooth ".[86]
14. " Or have ye not read in the law, how that on the sabbath days the priests in the temple profane the sabbath and are blameless?".[87]
15. " That in the mouth of two or three witnesses every word may be established ".[88]
16. " For this is my blood of the new testament ".[89] Surely symbolic both in the Book of Exodus and in Matthew's Gospel.
17. " And as Moses lifted up the serpent in the wilderness, even so must the Son of man be lifted up ".[90]

On no fewer than 32 occasions, or 17 if the reduplications are all omitted, Jesus either directly quoted, or directly referred to the Pentateuch as authoritative. He expressly confirmed the ten commandments by reiteration, albeit in condensed form, and He emphasised more than once, as the two most important commandments, the love of the Lord God and the love of neighbour—directly quoting in each case.

The effect of the rise and spread of Christianity through the world has been to carry the Old Testament for veneration along with the New Testament, so that where the name of Christ has come to be honoured so also has the name of Moses and of those who, as lesser prophets, arose within His shadow to guide and direct the people of Israel. No parallel can be found in history of such an effect, where the newer religion not merely does not overthrow the old but does its utmost to ensure that the sacred scriptures of that religion are read and venerated alongside its own. It would be difficult to imagine a greater service that could have been done by Christ for Moses, a far greater service than could ever have been achieved by the avowed followers of Moses on their own.

Abrogation of the Dispensation of Moses

When Jesus cursed the figtree He performed a symbolic act of abrogation of the dispensation of Moses.[91]

In one sense the fruit of the dispensation of Moses was the civilisation which reached its zenith under David and Solomon. An Israelite was at that time distinguished above all others of the region for his integrity, for his righteousness of outlook and judgment, for his faith in the one true God. The wealth of the region to quite an extent revolved round the culture and civilisation of the people of Israel. The Queen of Sheba did not think it beneath her to visit Solomon the Wise, and the fame of Israel spread to such an extent that during subsequent centuries Greek philosophers made journeys to sit at the feet of the Wise men of Israel from whom in due course they introduced a form of monotheism and belief in the immortality of the soul into the Greek schools. One of the greatest of all the Greek philosophers, Socrates, certainly made such a visit and was convinced of the rightness of these teachings to such an extent that he preferred death by hemlock, prescribed after condemnation by his fellow Athenians, to recantation or even flight to another land.

Although archaeologists have been able to trace some signs of the greatness of the civilisation of David and Solomon in terms of architecture and art, the chief mark of that civilisation was literary as may be seen from the Psalms of David and the great works of the law and the prophets. It is perhaps not surprising that the reflection to the west of the pervasive spirit of the dispensation of Moses also took a largely literary form, though in the Greek civilisation high achievements in architecture, sculpture and painting were also attained. There may even be a clue here to the phenomenon of Homer whose epic poems, the Iliad and the Odyssey, are the earliest pieces of European literature, yet by general consent rank among the most perfect of their kind.

In another sense the fruit of the dispensation of Moses was Jesus Himself, the perfect man, product of the religion of Moses but also, unlike other men, linked directly and indissolubly with the Godhead in such a way that He had full innate intuitive consciousness of all reality and supremely focussed the divine attributes in His own radiant spirit. Innately perfect though He was, Jesus yet was restricted by the conditions of the age and the limitations of the environment of understanding and knowledge. The tree of humanity could only grow at the pace decreed by divine wisdom and in its relative immaturity could only absorb so much and no more of the light, the truth and the knowledge of God.

In a third sense the fruits of the dispensation of Moses were the souls who recognised the prophethood, the divinity, in Jesus, responded to His call and through their response changed the whole planet, by their self-sacrificial lives through which they spread the glorious Word of God given them through Jesus. All those who acknowledged belief in Jesus during His lifetime had been born into the faith of Moses.

After the cursing of the figtree, although great individuals were yet to come from among the people of Israel who contributed to the cultural and intellectual achievements of the human race, and although the Jewish people sustained a depth of faith that has been an example to the world, yet no further fruit has appeared

91

from the ancient tree of their religion, in the sense of social progress, of healing the social ailments of the community, of great spiritual advance and understanding of the purpose of God, of spreading the knowledge and love of God among the peoples and nations of the planet. The life stream, or spirit of the age, had become channelled in a different channel, that of Christianity.

❌ Specifically, Jesus changed very little of the teachings of Moses ｡ He did however alter the law of divorce,[92] interpret the law of the sabbath more leniently[93] and through His authorised disciples He abrogated the law of circumcision[94] and almost totally removed the prohibitions on forbidden foods.[95] He also gave fresh point, content and depth of meaning to each of the ten great commandments.

*   *   *   *   *

For those who like to have their references handy, the following are given so that the reader may if he wishes study the actual extent of the changes He made:

Divorce: Mk. 10: 2-12, Matt. 19: 3-12, Matt. 5:31-32, Luke 16: 18.

Sabbath: Mk. 2:23-28, 3: 2-5, Matt. 12: 1-8, Luke 6: 1-10, 13:10-17, 14: 1-6, Jn. 7: 22-23.

Circumcision: Jn. 7:22-23, Acts 15: 1-29.

Food Laws: Acts 10: 9-17, 28, 15: 29.

Chapter 11

PERSPECTIVE AND REALITY

God's essential reality is and has always been concealed from and inaccessible to His creation. God created man because He was aware that He loved him and loved the process of creating him. Because He loved him God created man with the capacity to reflect Him, as a mirror reflects the image of what is before it. Because He loved him God made known to man His own perfections, His own beauty, so that man could respond to it and through his response could come to reflect that beauty, those perfections. The response He called love; the degree of response, or reflection of His own image, He called life. God being in Himself the Source, the Quintessence and the Sum of all life, to know God and to reflect His attributes is to enter more and more fully into life. Man's creation and its purpose constitutes this process, emerging and evolving from lifelessness, by degrees to ever higher levels of life.

⟨Man, in this context, is both the individual person, male or female, and the collective entity, human society or mankind as a whole.⟩

⟨God's primary attribute is justice. All men were created from the same dust, the same substance. None has a right to set himself above another.⟩

Man was brought forth by God's command from nothingness, given existence from the essence of knowledge, and moulded from the clay of love. Every atom and the essence of all created things were ordained by God for man's training, indeed everything in the universe except the human heart which He reserved for Himself.

Man's primary needs were provided for before he became aware that he needed them. A mother's milk for nurture, eyes for watchfulness and loving hearts to care for him are there for him before each child is born.

Man, however, passes through life in this world but once. He has but one chance to seize to develop his inner reality by his own efforts and self-mastery. Though capable of soaring to illimitable heights man is prone to temptation and may swiftly fall, brought low by the attraction of earthly transient things, the vain show, the mirage of worldly interests. The dust of the world comes to obscure the radiance of the heart's mirror, the slumber of sensuality numbs the spirit, the rust of ungodliness corrodes the finer faculties.[1]

93

So far is the Creator exalted above His creation that comprehension is impossible and direct access totally barred. The process of creation and redemption is made possible through the chosen Vehicles of His Word, Who expound His purpose and reveal His truth. These beings focus God's attributes to man, guide him on the true path and reveal the degree of knowledge of God to which evolving mankind is able to aspire. Mediating the Holy rays of God's Spirit They renew the ancient eternal faith of God and re-establish man's grasp on the cord of God's covenant with His creation, They have different names, different specific missions, different prescriptions for man's changing ailments but They carry the same authority, effect the same response, evince the same purpose—the peace, happiness and tranquillity of man's hearts, the right ordering of human affairs, the priority of the spiritual life, the advancement of the interests of society as a whole.

❝ People think religion is confined to an edifice, to be worshipped at an altar. In reality it is an attitude towards divinity which is reflected through life ❞[2]

Surely Jesus implied this when He said, " The first of all the commandments is, ' Hear, O Israel; the Lord our God is one Lord: and thou shalt love the Lord thy God with all thy heart, and with all thy soul, and with all thy mind, and with all thy strength ': this is the first commandment. And the second is like, namely this, " Thou shalt love thy neighbour as thyself.' There is none other commandment greater than these ".[3]

All His injunctions, His imperatives, His precepts, deriving as they did from the Son of the living God, are clear guides for action, attitude and behaviour in practical affairs in daily life, every day. Difficult at times they may be, but prayerful sincere attempts to carry them out are necessary for man to create his own self, his own future. They are impossible unless man realises the supreme living Authority behind them, the sustaining grace of that Authority in the face of mountains of difficulty, the end result towards which they are directed.

Man needs to know his own self and those things that lead to eternal honour or eternal abasement. None of them can be carried out vicariously, by any other except himself. The injunctions to follow, to teach, to practise, to love God, to love one another, to defer to others, to seek the kingdom, to understand etc. were addressed to ordinary people and were intended for every one, for all time and for everywhere. Most certainly they were not intended only for special people, for a special day or in a special place.

" This has been the mission of all the divine messengers, to make man conscious of his eternal part." " The masters of all time have suffered for none other than this, that fleshly veils might be rent asunder and reality become manifest ".[4]

No sign can come from a non-existent thing. Since clearly we are aware of the signs and influence of the great ones of the past we know too that their true reality is existent, indestructible. It is wholly unscientific to suppose that existence can ever become non-existence. The animating principle, man's inner reality, clearly exists: each one of us is aware of it in himself. Positive qualities of the soul are intangible, yet they exist. Kindness, generosity, courage, tolerance are such qualities. How can these things cease to exist?

The whole tenor of the Holy Gospels takes on a different dimension, a different and immeasurably deeper content and significance if they are pondered with the eye of spirituality and with the humility of knowing that they cannot be exhausted in their meaning and value. For that is what is implicit in the fact that they enshrine the Word of God. There are many specific passages— e.g. the reply to the Sadducees,[5] the parable of Dives and Lazarus,[6] the appearance of Moses and Elijah at the transfiguration,[7] the assurance to the thief on the cross,[8]—which indicate a greater explicitness, but in fact every part of the Gospels should be seen as conveying a glorious sense of spiritual immortal purpose. The quality of life enjoined has little object if it ceases with physical death. The entire purpose of creation is of small moment if it merely culminates in a few brief days of more or less sensible activity in a mortal span. The justice of God, the life and death of His Chosen Ones have but trivial meaning and would be impossible to accept if they were confined to this physical realm for their effects.

No, the world of the spirit surrounds this physical world, interpenetrates and permeates it. The world of the spirit is the eternal realm of reality into which we can be born again and become qualified for active service, if we so choose and if we make an effort.

◄Man is not created for the life of this ephemeral world— nay, rather, is he created for the acquirement of infinite perfections, for the attainment to the sublimity of the world of humanity, to be drawn nigh unto the divine threshold, and to sit on the throne of everlasting sovereignty ".►

◄" His Holiness Jesus Christ gave His life upon the cross for the unity of mankind. Those who believed in Him likewise sacrificed life, honour, possessions, family, everything, that this human world might be released from the hell of discord, emnity and strife. His foundation was the oneness of humanity. Only a few were attracted to Him ► . .

"Through His death and teachings we have entered into His kingdom. His essential teaching was the unity of mankind and attainment of supreme human virtues through love. He came to establish the kingdom of peace and everlasting life. Can you find in His words any justification for discord and enmity? The purpose of His life and glory of His death was to set mankind free from the sin of strife, war and bloodshed. The great nations of the world boast that their laws and civilisation are based upon the religion of Christ. Why then do they make war upon each other? The kingdom of Christ cannot be upheld by destroying and disobeying it. The banners of His armies cannot lead the forces of satan . . .

" No less bitter is the conflict between sects and denominations. Christ was a divine centre of unity and love. Whenever discord prevails instead of unity, wherever hatred and antagonism take the place of love and spiritual fellowship, antichrist reigns instead of Christ. Who is right in these controversies and hatreds between the sects? Did Christ command them to love or to hate each other? He loved even His enemies and prayed in the hour of His crucifixion for those who killed Him. Therefore to be a Christian is not merely to bear the name of Christ and say ' I belong to a Christian government.' To be a real Christian is to be a servant in His cause and kingdom, to go forth under His banner of peace and love toward all mankind, to be self-sacrificing and obedient, to become quickened by the breaths of the Holy Spirit, to be mirrors reflecting the radiance of the divinity of Christ, to be fruitful trees in the garden of His planting, to refresh the world by the water of life of His teachings; in all things to be like Him and filled with the spirit of His love ".[10]

" The only true explainer of the book of God is the Holy Spirit, for no two minds are alike, no two can comprehend alike, no two can speak alike. That is to say, from the mere human standpoint of interpretation there could be neither truth nor agreement ".[11]

Jesus did all that could be done at that time to make man aware of the way, the truth and the life; His way, the only way for the soul of man to follow so as to fulfil the purpose of his creation, the only truth of eternal importance, the only life with real meaning.

Chapter 12

PROGRESSIVE REVELATION

Each individual human growing up passes through infancy, childhood, early youth and adolescence before attaining adult maturity. Increasingly, everywhere, these stages of growth are marked by distinct educational steps, kindergarten, primary school, secondary school, and college respectively. During these stages the human is subject to guidance; afterwards, assumed mature, each takes responsibility for his own further development.

Similarly, human society, since prehistoric times, has been passing through stages of social organisation represented by the family, the tribe, the city state, the nation, each successively more complex. It is now entering the universal stage, the highest attainable on the planet, comparable to adulthood and post college education for the individual.

Just as the individual growing human cannot educate himself, so human society requires an Educator.

The Educators of human society are the Messengers or Manifestations of God, Who successively renewed God's religion, widened the application of the law of love and reciprocity towards one's neighbour and revealed social regulations and doctrines appropriate to a growing society's changing needs. Thus Abraham, Moses, Jesus and Muhammad (as Krishna, Zoroaster, Buddha and others elsewhere), in the heartland of the planet, successively educated human society. The law of love, the ethical and spiritual teachings have remained constant throughout; the non-essential regulations and doctrines were inevitably varied. For example, death by stoning for adultery or the death penalty for breaking the law on the sabbath prescribed by Moses could not now be applied

These Educators were identical in the Source of Their inspiration, in Their motives and purposes, but complementary and progressive in Their missions. The quality of Their early followers was comparable; the spiritual impetus They imparted generated in each case a great advance in art, science, culture and civilisation.

' Abdu'l-Bahá once said, " This universe is created by a great law which decrees that the tree bring forth certain definite fruit." The " fruit " of this planet is the human race. The fruit is perfected when it is ripe and sweet. According to a law of nature, the will of God, human society therefore attains full maturity through unification on a global scale. Just as in earlier stages, so the final stage of the " fruit's " growth can be fully effected and the sweetness of

97

G

harmonious mutual reciprocity and love be established only through a Divine Educator. This stage was anticipated by all past Educators as the mighty consummation of the plan of God to which Their missions were directly linked.

Like Suns of Truth in the heaven of the spirit, these Educators provided a direction for men's hearts and vital food for their souls, progressively intensifying the potency at each rising until with Bahá'u'lláh " all truth " has been revealed. Future Suns of Truth, as They appear, each with His own book, each fulfilling, confirming, abrogating, judging, instituting, heralding, will sustain and further intensify the sweetness of the " fruit " of the tree of humanity brought to full ripeness by Bahá'u'lláh.

Conclusion

Surely now we have a fully coherent picture of the Christianity of Jesus. Born in mysterious circumstances to a poor maiden of Israel, descendant of Abraham, and brought up in the house of a carpenter himself descended from the royal line of David, Jesus early showed the promise of His inner spiritual Reality, a promise that was made explicit when His mission began at the time of His baptism in the river Jordan, at the age of about thirty, by John the Baptist.

After withdrawal for communion in the wilderness with the glorious spirit of His Father, an event which He later expounded as a warning to the community of His followers, Jesus called twelve to arise and follow Him, expounded the ancient sacred scriptures in the meeting places of the land, healed many of unbelief, wayward attitudes and perverse behaviour, taught His message more and more widely, instructed His disciples who grew to know, love and understand Him till the moment of recognition of His station as the promised Messiah, accepted betrayal, interrogation by authority both religious and secular, condemnation, crucifixion.

So well had He taught the eleven men and three or four women that despite initial confusion caused by the divine test of His ignominious end, they realised, with an opening of the eye of insight, that He that came from heaven, had lived in heaven while among them, had not in truth died on the cross but was ever-living, a vital eternal influence for man's guidance. Even the doubter was overwhelmed with proof through his testing the truth of the inward vision. This experience was so overwhelming that it moved the disciples to their supreme act of consultation when at Pentecost inspired by the Holy Spirit, they resolved to go and preach the gladtidings throughout the earth. Jesus Himself however had been withdrawn beyond the reach of the inner eye to the realm of the placeless, to heaven.

Jesus completed and fulfilled many of the Old Testament prophecies; confirmed most of the principal teachings of Moses; abrogated the Mosaic dispensation; judged the age, condemning it for its servitude to tradition, its hypocrisy, its superstition and its materialism; instituted His own era of peaceful spiritual sovereignty over the hearts of men; heralded the coming of the Kingdom of God on earth, giving signs by which its coming would be recognised in a more explicit way even than the books of the prophets of old.

By example and by precept He taught those who came to recognise Him, to live a life of radiant spirituality, of prayer and fasting, of sacrifice and love, of unity and harmony, giving all that was needful for keeping this life pure and harmonious, especially calling on them to keep Him ever in mind, to overcome their own selfish propensities, to take to themselves His perfections, to maintain their unity. Peter was singled out for his faith and understanding revealed to him by the Father in heaven, a faith and understanding that was to be the basis of the law of His church, His community of believers. All who turned to Him could become sons of God, could and should preach His word, could heal the sick at heart, could baptise the converted.

When the gladtidings of the coming Kingdom of God were preached throughout the planet, when the control of Israel by foreigners had ceased, when Daniel's prophecy of 2300 years (from B.C. 457) had come to pass, then would the Kingdom of God arrive, with His own return. First a Comforter, then His own return, then the Lord of the vineyard Himself, and all men would come within one fold acknowledging the voice of one shepherd.

So intense, so quintessentially pure, were the teachings of Jesus that His words would never pass away, even though the ' heavens ' of other dispensations came and went and the ' earth ' of human understanding failed. Never to be outmoded, the Word of God, present in the plan of God from the beginning of time and made explicit through Christ, would shine out resplendent so that Christ would forever sit on the right hand of the Father even when the Father had come Himself to take over and rule the planet, His vineyard. True, the believers would be deceived; true, there were shepherds who would be wolves in sheep's clothing; true, there would be tares innumerable in the wheat at the time of the harvest; true, the time of the end would come when nearly all had fallen asleep, heedless of the Word, unable to hear it; but there would be some alert—as there had not been in Sodom and Gomorrha—and for their sake the days of trial would be shortened and the long-promised Kingdom of God brought into being to develop over the surface of the earth until the earth at long last reflected the perfections of the Kingdom of God in heaven to the utmost of its inherent capacity.

Christ's Promise Fulfilled

The great promise of Christ to come again among men is referred to in over 250 separate passages[1] of the New Testament. Christ Himself referred more than 90 times to His own return.

To suppose, as some do, that this promise was fulfilled at Pentecost is to fly in the face of many clear references to it as a future event made by Peter, Paul and James[2] long after Pentecost.

The disciples spoke often of Christ's promise and were eager to understand the conditions under which He would return, the signs that would mark His coming. So frequent are the references that it is no wonder that so many Chritians for centuries have been filled with millennial zeal, a zeal which reached a climax in the early years of the fifth decade of the nineteenth century.

The purpose of the mission of the Lord Christ Himself, as we have already discovered was sixfold: to fulfil the scriptures, to confirm souls in the eternal faith of God, to judge those who professed belief in Moses, to abrogate or adjust the law and the teachings to conform to the needs of the new age, to initiate His own spiritual reign over the hearts of men, to anticipate the coming of the Lord of Hosts, His own return in the glory of the Father.

Christ gave three clear indications of His return: 1, His gospels would be preached in all the world for a witness[3]; 2, the times of the Gentiles would be fulfilled[4]; 3, the " abomination of desolation " spoken of by Daniel the prophet would be seen.[5]

In the early years of the nineteenth century there seems to have occurred the greatest outburst of missionary enthusiasm and activity since the apostolic era. The British and Foreign Bible Society was formed in 1804, the American Bible Society in 1816. From 50 languages in 1804 the translations of the Bible rapidly grew to several hundred. In 1842 treaty ports in China were opened to commerce and to missions; in 1844 Turkey agreed to recognise the right of Muslims to become Christians, the South African Mission was established, Tibet was entered for the first time. By 1844 the gospel of Christ had entered every continent and Christian missions had begun activities among the African peoples in East Africa.

" The times of the Gentiles " clearly means the period of time during which Jerusalem would be held in the power of aliens, non-Jews or Gentiles, during which the Jews themselves would be exiled from their homeland or held in subjection. Forty years after the crucifixion of Christ the Jews were conquered, scattered, exiled and Jerusalem destroyed by the Roman Titus, an event which was duplicated, but even more completely, about sixty years later by the Roman Emperor Hadrian. The Romans were thus the first Gentiles to tread down the holy city of Jerusalem. They were followed by the Muslims who conquered Palestine some 500 years later in 637 A.D. and strictly excluded the Jews from their homeland until, by the Edict of Toleration dated 21st March 1844, the Muslims under the leadership of Turkey were compelled by the Western Powers, notably Britain, to grant religious toleration to all peoples within their borders and the Jews, for the first time for over 1200 years, were guaranteed the right to return to Israel.

Now the 21st March 1844 is exactly 2300 years after the 21st March 457 B.C. and that was the day on which Ezra states that he left Babylon in compliance with the decree given in the 7th year of the reign of Artaxerxes. From 457 B.C. to the date of Christ's crucifixion was 490 years, which is represented as 70 weeks or 490 days in the prophecy of Daniel,[6] and from 457 B.C. to the birth of Christ there were 456 years, leaving 1844 as the fulfilment of

Daniel's prophecy regarding Christ's second coming. It was clearly to these words of Daniel, in the 8th chapter of his book, that Christ Himself referred, " How long shall be the vision concerning the daily sacrifice, and the abomination of desolation, to give the sanctuary and the host to be trodden under foot? And he said unto me, ' Unto two thousand and three hundred days; then shall the sanctuary be cleansed ' "[7]

Thus by 1844 the word of Christ had been preached in all the world, the times of the Gentiles had been fulfilled and the prophecy of Daniel had come to pass.

In 1844 in Persia, the Elam of the Old Testament[8] the Báb announced to the 18 disciples who had sought Him out that He was the Promised One come to fulfil the scriptures of old. He sent those disciples, whom He called Letters of the Living, out to teach throughout the world, reminding them that they were the bearers of the name of God for that day and that their deeds and their demeanour must demonstrate this.[9]

The Báb in an extraordinary way matched the ministry of Christ. For six years, three of them in prison, He aroused the peoples, expounded the scriptures, wrote His Tablets and books, established His laws, abrogated the religion of His time, announced the coming of One yet greater than Himself. Like Christ, the Báb was youthful, being only 25 at the start of His ministry, was known for His meekness and loving kindness, performed healing miracles, challenged the conventions, laws and rites of the religion into which He was born, condemned the widespread corruption, shamed the people by the purity of His life, was opposed by the religious leaders of the land, was heaped with indignities, forcibly brought to trial before the government authorities, scourged after interrogation, proceeded first in triumph then in suffering through the streets of the city where he was to be slain, was paraded publicly and heaped with humiliation on His way to martyrdom, spoke words of promise to one who was to die with Him, was martyred publicly, was lacerated by soldiers at the time of dying, remained ignominiously suspended before the eyes of an unfriendly multitude.

As with Christ, the Báb's ministry was brief, darkness covered the land after His martyrdom, His body came finally into the hands of loving friends, only a handful of followers were present at the time of His death, an outstanding woman follower played a dramatic part in helping the disciples to turn their faces from the past and look to the future, confusion and despair seized His followers after His passing, His disciples were charged to convey His message to the ends of the earth and effectively carried this out.

As with Christ, a mighty religion had been abrogated and its leaders were later to be wholly abased. As with Christ, the early believers in the Báb joyfully gave their lives by the thousand for His love.

In 1853, nine years after the Báb's declaration and as promised by Him, the " third woe ", greatest of them all, coming quickly as foretold in the 11th chapter of Revelations,[10] began with the commencement of Bahá'u'lláh's ministry, in a dark dungeon at Tihran, also in Persia. Banished from His homeland, imprisoned in 'Akká in Palestine never to return, Bahá'u'lláh called upon the " husbandmen " of His vineyard[11] to render account. He wrote to the rulers and religious leaders of the world and was rejected. Those " husbandmen ", ever since, have steadily been dispossessed, while mankind has been forced to suffer the consequences in disillusionment, demoralisation and despair with wars unprecedented and an uprooting of whole peoples. Thus the Lord of the vineyard Himself came to lead mankind into all truth,[12] yet like a thief in the night[13] unrecognised, unnoticed.

The tree of life has put forth fresh leaves[14] all over the world. People of every religion, race and class with steadily increasing numbers have been awakening to the brilliant truths of the age which Bahá'u'lláh disclosed to mankind. Bahá'u'lláh with innate knowledge, unhelped by any schooling, focussed the spirit of the age in His great teachings and gave us 'Abdu'l-Bahá, His eldest Son, the St. Peter of the age with written authority and supreme exemplary perfection of character, to sustain the unity and harmony of the renewed Faith of God. Truth to be sought out without restraint of tradition or superstition, the consciousness of the oneness of the entire human race, the essential oneness of the divne religions, elimination of all prejudices, equal rights for women, compulsory education for all, an international auxiliary language, the harmony of religion with science and reason, the pre-eminent importance of justice and religion in human affairs, abolition of extremes of wealth and poverty, the inculcation of global peace as man's supreme goal, the institution of a Supreme Tribunal to adjudicate on national disputes, obedience to government, spiritual harmony in family life—these are the principal rays of the life giving spirit of the age brought by Bahá'u'lláh.

Christ warned of false prophets coming in sheep's clothing,[15] of persons expounding in His name,[16] of the tares in the field of wheat ready for harvest,[17] of the leaven of the hypocritical Pharisees and the grasping Herodians,[18] whose influence would be such that, with the great tribulations at this time of the end of His age, " there should no flesh be saved: but for the elect's sake those days shall be shortened."[19]

Christ promised a Comforter[20]: Muhammad came to renew His teachings and to offer man the way to organise by nations as an intermediate stage before the possibility existed of organising internationally. Christ said He Himself would return[21]: the Báb's ministry duplicated His own, point by point. Christ said the Lord of the vineyard,[22] the Spirit of Truth,[23] would come: Bahá'u'lláh has brought all the love, the law and the truth we need for at least a

103

thousand years. Yet each is essentially one and the same, each perfectly expressed the word of God for His day and age.

Christ prayed, " Thy kingdom come, Thy will be done, on earth as it is in heaven."[24] Bahá'u'lláh shows how to make this prophecy effective, for the institutions He has created will really and for the first time be an administration of the people, for the people, *by God*. That is why they are known as Houses of Justice and their elected members as the trustees of God.

The Most Great Justice emerging from the welter of this confused, despairing age when the Universal House of Justice has been formed and is developing, will in turn lead on to the Most Great Peace and finally the Golden Age of man. The words of Christ will never pass away[25] for they herald this grand culmination of the handiwork of God. Bahá'u'lláh said, ' Blessed is the man who, with a face beaming with light, hath turned towards Him (Christ)'[26] and " Be thou assured in thyself that verily he who turns away from this Beauty (Bahá'u'lláh) hath also turned away from the Messengers of the past and showeth pride towards God from all eternity to all eternity."[27]

Thus the great Covenant made by God with Abraham, and thrice repeated, that in His seed shall all the nations of the earth be blessed,[28] will once again be fulfilled. The nations of the earth have been blessed by the appearance of Moses and His great laws, by Jesus and His radiant spirituality, by Muhammad and the civilisation that was inspired by the mighty Quran, and the Covenant was fulfilled in the seed of Abraham by Sarah[29] and by Hagar.[30] But Abraham had a third wife, Keturah,[31] by whom He had offspring, and the word of God never goes forth in vain.[32] Bahá'u'lláh is of the line of Abraham by His third wife, Keturah. He is surely destined to effect a reconciliation between the followers of Moses, of Jesus, and of Muhammad, making of them all one nation in a world at peace.

At long last the great prophecy of Isaiah will be complete, for Bahá'u'lláh is "the rod out of the stem of Jesse,"[33] the man-child given us "upon whose shoulder shall be the government, whose name shall be called Wonderful, Counsellor, the mighty God, the everlasting Father, the Prince of Peace, whose government and whose peace shall be established with judgment and with justice from henceforth even for ever."[34]

Christ called His disciples to be fishers of men,[35] individual souls. Christ clearly distinguished Himself over and over again from the Father who sent Him,[36] who had knowledge,[37] powers[38] and perfections[39] He did not possess. Christ disclaimed sovereignty over the world saying His Kingdom was not of this world.[40] The peace Christ left was given not as the world giveth,[41] indeed Christ expressly stated that He had not come to send peace on earth, but a sword.[42]

104

Bahá'u'lláh is Christ returned in the glory of the Father[43] (Bahá'u'lláh means Glory of God), come to quicken mankind as a whole,[44] to unify all the diverse peoples of the earth who have been as wolves, leopards and lions so that they will lie down with the lambs, the kids and the calves.[45] Bahá'u'lláh has brought the institutions for establishing a just government under divine inspiration. In course of creation now are the new heavens and the new earth;[46] the holy city, new Jerusalem, prepared as a bride adorned for her husband, is already come down from God out of heaven.[47] Soon* indeed shall the former things, the first heaven and the first earth, have passed away entirely.[48] Soon* shall be seen that " they shall not hurt nor destroy in all my holy mountain: for the earth shall be full of the knowledge of the Lord, as the waters cover the sea.[49] The foundation of His government has been laid in nearly every country of the world; the organic structure of that government is developing faster each year; the Christ-promised kingdom of God is already with us established albeit still in embryo form so that His will shall be done on earth as it is in heaven.[50]

* Footnote: In the time span of the life history of the planet " Soon " means within the next few generations, to be measured in decades instead of thousands of years.

Appendix A

MARK'S GOSPEL

The Gospel Story

The story of the ministry of Jesus Christ set out in Mark's Gospel, which is acknowledged by general agreement to be the earliest of the synoptic gospels, may be summarised as follows:

After baptism in the Jordan near Nazareth by John the Baptist, Jesus spent forty days apart ' in the wilderness ', then moved to Galilee to proclaim His mission, called Simon and Andrew, James and John, two pairs of brothers, to follow Him and proceeded to Capernaum where he taught in the synagogue and quietened a distraught soul. He then went to the house of Simon and Andrew whose mother He healed of a fever. After healing others He proceeded to preach in synagogues throughout Galilee and healed many more, notably a leper(1). Jesus again went to Capernaum and many gathered to hear Him; a man bed-ridden with palsy was brought to Him and healed; Jesus called Levi (Matthew), a customs officer, and sat to a meal with tax collectors and other unorthodox people, an action which provoked questions from scribes and Pharisees as did the failure of the disciples of Jesus to observe the customary fasts or strict recognition of the law of the sabbath, questions to which Jesus gave effective replies(2). Jesus healed a man's withered hand on the sabbath under further protest from the Pharisees who promptly consulted with the Herodians about action to take. Jesus then withdrew to the sea of Galilee with His disciples where a multitude followed Him; after taking ship, speaking to the people and healing many, Jesus went up a mountain and selected twelve disciples—Simon whom He renamed Peter, James and John (sons of Zebedee), Andrew, Philip, Bartholomew, Matthew (Levi), Thomas, James (son of Alpheus), Thaddeus, Simon the Zealot, and Judas Iscariot. They went into a house and crowds gathered to throng Him. Jesus refuted certain scribes from Jerusalem when they suggested that He effected His results through the powers of darkness. His mother and brothers came to see Him(3).

Jesus again taught by the seaside, taking ship and speaking to crowds on the shore. The parable of the sower scattering the seed (or word of God) and the results He explained at their request to His disciples and He compared the kingdom of God to a seed sprouting and growing and also to a grain of mustard seed. At evening He sent away the crowds and passed over the sea by ship sleeping on the way; when a storm arose which alarmed the disciples, they roused Him and He rebuked the wind and there was calm, thus raising questions in their minds(4). They landed in the country of the Gadarenes and were met by a man who lived on his own in the mountains and among the tombs, possessed by an untamable spirit. This man recognised Jesus as the Son of God and asked Him not to torment him, but Jesus quietened him and permitted the various influences that possessed him to enter a herd of swine nearby which promptly rushed down into the sea and were drowned; the man himself Jesus instructed to go home and tell his friends of the circumstances. Jesus then recrossed the sea and was met by many, among whom one of the synagogue's rulers named Jairus implored Him to heal his daughter who was dying at home. While on the way to Jairus' home Jesus healed a woman who had touched His clothes believing she might thus be cured of a long standing ailment. Although people came and told Jesus He was too late He yet went into Jairus' house and aroused his daughter to full health again(5).

Jesus then returned home again. On the sabbath He taught in the synagogue causing offence to some who remembered Him as the son of a humble carpenter and His family living among them. Thus largely frustrated Jesus went out and about in the nearby villages and sent out His disciples in pairs with instructions to travel light and live simply and to teach and preach repentance. These actions alarmed King Herod who thought it must be John the Baptist come again whom he had had beheaded to please his daughter and his wife. On the return of the disciples Jesus took them apart by ship to rest in the country, but they were spotted as they went and many people rushed round the sea to catch up with them. Jesus taught them till late at night and then requested the disciples to feed them. By means of five loaves and two fishes the crowd of some 5,000 were satisfied and twelve basketfuls of fragments were gathered up afterwards. Jesus then got in the boat and passed over to Bethsaida and thence to pray on a mountain. At evening He saw the disciples who had taken to the sea again, toiling away rowing against the wind; He then walked out to meet them over the sea to encourage them: then the wind dropped and they came to Gennesaret where the people at once gathered up all the sick persons they could find for Him to heal(6).

Some Pharisees and scribes from Jerusalem came to visit Jesus and noticed that His disciples were eating without having washed their hands, a practice contrary to traditional custom. They challenged Jesus about this and were promptly denounced for hypocrisy in putting man-made traditions above the commandments of God. Jesus illustrated His retort with a number of examples notably the way they had circumvented the command of filial piety. Jesus went on to state in effect that every good thing is of God and every evil thing from the selfish heart of man. Jesus then departed for the coasts of Tyre and Sidon where He wanted to obtain temporary concealment, but He was met by a Greek woman of Syrophenician origin who begged Him to heal her daughter of a devil; she humbly but wittily persisted even when Jesus said His mission was first for the children of Israel, and was rewarded. Jesus then returned via the coasts of Decapolis to the sea of Galilee and healed a deaf man with a speech impediment; despite requests to keep the matter quiet, the people spread the news abroad(7). Again the crowds were great, numbering about 4,000, and had nothing to eat and again Jesus required the disciples to feed them with the seven loaves and a few small fishes that they had; this time there were seven basketfuls of fragments afterwards. Jesus and His disciples then took ship and crossed to Dalmanutha where they were met by Pharisees who requested a sign from Him as proof of His greatness but Jesus refused them and departed by ship once more to the other side of the sea. The disciples now had only one loaf between them but Jesus warned them to watch out for the ' leaven ' of the Pharisees and the Herodians, recalling the recent feeding of the multitude to help them see that He did not mean the leaven that went into the making of bread. They came to Bethsaida and were brought a blind man whom Jesus healed and again asked to keep the matter quiet. Jesus and His disciples then departed for the town of Caesarea Philippi and on the way Jesus asked the disciples who people thought He was. The disciples answered variously, but to the same question put to themselves Peter replied, " Thou art the Christ." Jesus then forewarned them of His sombre destiny, and when Peter strongly protested he drew upon himself the sternest rebuke ever uttered, " Get thee behind me, Satan." Jesus thereupon clarified the meaning of the true service in His cause and alluded to His own return in the glory of the Father(8).

Six days later Jesus took Peter, James and John with Him apart up a mountain and was transfigured before them in the presence of Moses and Elijah. Peter proposed to set up habitations (tabernacles) for each of them and they heard a voice from out of a cloud that overshadowed them, " This is my beloved Son, hear him." At that the three disciples found themselves alone with Jesus who charged them to keep it to themselves until the Son of man was risen from the dead. They then asked why the scribes said that Elijah must first come, and Jesus explained. When they rejoined the others they found them thronged with people having been unable to heal a child of a deaf and dumb condition. Jesus told them that all things were possible to a believer and on urgent insistence for help by the child's father healed the boy; He later mentioned to the disciples that prayer and fasting were needed for this sort of healing. He and the disciples then left for Capernaum and Jesus again referred to His own sombre destiny and asked what the disciples had discussed between them on the way. He indicated that he who would be first among them must show the utmost degree of servitude to all and took a child and explained that whoever received such a child in His name received both Jesus and Him that sent Jesus. He further told them that people were either for Him or against Him whether or not they were recognised followers, depending on their actions. He warned against those who were recognised followers, even of high rank, if they offended or obstructed the work, commanded that they be cast out and described their fate. He enjoined His followers to retain their unity, harmony and faith(9).

Jesus then went to the coast of Judaea on the other side of Jordan and was approached by the Pharisees who asked Him about the legality of divorce which Moses had permitted according to form; Jesus replied that the equal division into two sexes was a creational one, that marriage entailed the propriety of leaving one's parents and involved a complete union. Marriage as a decree of God was not subject to man's power to dissolve. To His disciples privately He added that to divorce and marry another automatically entailed committing adulturery, a breach of one of the ten commandments.

When some young children were brought for His blessing Jesus insisted that they be allowed to come to Him since they were the hope of the future Kingdom of God and indeed entrance to that kingdom depended on its prior acceptance in the spirit of a little child.

As Jesus was proceeding on His way again a man came running up and asked how he might inherit eternal life, and averred that he knew and observed the commandments, but when Jesus asked him to sell up, give to the poor and follow Him, he went away sadly for he was rich. Jesus commented that rich people find it hard to enter the kingdom of God, harder than a camel to pass through a needle's eye, though of course with God all things were possible. Peter reminded Jesus that the disciples had abandoned everything and Jesus promised abundant blessings both in this world and in the world to come for such action.

Again they took the road for Jerusalem and Jesus again warned them of His own impending death. To James and John, sons of Zebedee, who asked to be allowed to sit on either side of Him in His ' glory ', He explained that this was not in His power to grant though they could drink of the same cup and experience the same baptism. When the other disciples were upset over his conversation, Jesus mentioned that His followers must be different from secular authority since their preferment must arise from service in the same way as His own service, which was to death.

They reached Jericho and Jesus healed the blind beggar Bartimaeus, son of Timaeus, who recognised Him and importuned Him (10).

As they approached Jerusalem and reached Bethphage and Bethany by the mount of Olives, Jesus sent two disciples to requisition a colt from the village nearby. They brought the colt, put garments on it and Jesus rode down into Jerusalem while many spread garments and branches on the path and all cried ' Hosanna ', giving Him a triumphal ovation. Jesus entered the temple and at evening withdrew again to Bethany with the disciples. The next day, as they returned to Jerusalem, Jesus was hungry and cursed a figtree because it had nothing but leaves on it and the tree dried up from the roots. On reaching the temple again Jesus cleared the building of traffickers and money-changers, an action which aroused the fear of the scribes and chief priests and brought them to seek His destruction. At evening they withdrew again and Jesus used the example of the withered figtree to urge faith in God, prayer and forgiveness as the basis for action when nothing would be beyond their powers. They returned once more to Jerusalem and the chief priests, scribes and elders approached Jesus as He walked in the temple asking Him to state His authority for His actions. Jesus replied that if they would tell Him whether the baptism of John the Baptist was of heaven or of men He would tell them His authority, and thus a deadlock ensued (11).

At that point Jesus addressed to them the parable of the vineyard, the husbandmen, the treatment of the owner's servants and of his son, and the revenge the owner must take when he returned. The building material rejected by the secular builders would prove to be the keystone of the building. Aware that this was aimed at themselves they went away but sent some of the Pharisees and Herodians to try and trip Him up in discussion. In answer to their question as to the legality of paying tribute to Caesar, Jesus enjoined obedience as a true characteristic to be demonstrated according to circumstances secular or religious. In answer to Sadducees who asked Him about the relationship in the after life of a wife to seven brothers she had married successively as each died and left no heir, Jesus said that difference of sex had no connection with the spiritual realm and explained that God reigned over a realm of life, here and hereafter.

One of the scribes was attracted by Jesus' replies and asked Him which was the first of all the commandments to which Jesus answered by quoting Deuteronomy 6: 4-5 and Leviticus 19: 18 as the first and second commandments beyond all others, the true love of the one God and the love for neighbour as oneself. The scribe was deeply moved by this and Jesus told him he was not far from the kingdom of God.

While teaching in the temple, Jesus asked how the scribes could say that Christ was the son of David when David himself had said that the Lord had called his Lord to sit on His right hand until his enemies were conquered: how then could He be called David's son? He added that people should watch out for the hypocrisy of the scribes who set themselves apart by their mode of dress and expectation of preferment on both religious and social occasions, made long extempore prayers and exploited the poor.

As Jesus was watching contributions to the temple treasury He remarked of a poor widow who had put in a farthing that her contribution outweighed that of them all as she had given such a high proportion of her income (12).

As they emerged from the temple one of the disciples commented on the grandeur of the building, but Jesus foretold its total destruction. Then as they sat on the mount of Olives Peter, James, John and Andrew asked when this would occur. Jesus replied by warnings of deceitfulness in His name, of unprecedented strife and turmoil, calamities and trouble throughout the world, of persecution of the faithful and He gave them four signs of His coming again: (i) that His gospel must first be preached throughout the planet; (ii) that Daniel's ' abomination of desolation ' would dominate till the date fixed in the prophecy; (iii) that the sun, moon and stars of heaven—the laws of religion and the acknowledged exponents thereof—would be eclipsed or fall from authority; (iv) that the tree of religion would put forth fresh leaves. He even warned that so effective would prove the seduction of the false exposition of His message that many would be led astray and that the retribution would be so severe that unless the transition period were shortened by God's mercy for the sake of His true followers all mankind would perish. His return would be with invincible might and splendour, though concealed by the veils of a physical body as clouds concealed the sun; He would nevertheless be aided by many pure souls and would draw together into one world community people from all parts of the earth. He reminded them that His sayings were indestructible, that only the Father knew the exact time of the events, that the faithful should be alert and prayerful or they might be caught unawares (13).

Two days later there came the feast of the passover and of unleavened bread and the chief priests and the scribes plotted how to make an end of Jesus.

As Jesus was eating in the house of Simon the leper, in Bethany, a woman came and anointed His head with costly oil of spikenard from an alabaster box, an act which displeased some as they thought it a waste. But Jesus praised her act giving it a special significance in the light of His own impending end and promising her act immortality. But Judas Iscariot reacted by going to offer detrayal of Jesus to the chief priests who promised him a reward.

Jesus sent two disciples to follow through the arrangements for an upper room in Jerusalem where He and they could celebrate the passover, and that evening they all assembled there. As they were eating Jesus warned that one of those present eating with Him would betray Him: although by doing so that person fulfilled scripture, yet for him it would have been better if he had never existed. Jesus then broke bread and passed round the cup exhorting those present to eat and drink and imprint the occasion on their minds remembering

Him always and His new covenant with them to have faith in Him. He mentioned that He would not drink again of the fruit of the vine until He drank it fresh in the kingdom of God.

They then sang a hymn and went out to the mount of Olives where Jesus again warned them that they would be upset and confused because of impending events that night when He would be taken and struck down, but would rise again and precede them into Galilee. Peter objected that he could not be upset, but Jesus said he would in fact deny Him three times before the cock crowed twice.

They then went to a place called Gethsemane and Jesus told the disciples to stay while He went apart with Peter, James and John and prayed. He told the three to keep awake and prayed that the hour might pass and the testing time be taken away, but that the Father's will was to prevail. Three times He came back and found the three sleeping and warned them of temptation, acknowledging however that though their spirit was willing the flesh was weak— they were yet too unready and immature. Then He awakened them and Judas came up with an armed group from the chief priests, scribes and elders and went to Jesus and kissed Him, thereby indicating Whom they were to arrest. A scuffle ensued when a bystander drew his sword and cut off the ear of a servant of the high priest. Jesus remarked that though He was in the temple teaching by day yet they had come at night, armed, to arrest Him as if He were a thief. His followers fled, and a young man who had been close behind Him was grasped by the mob but escaped, leaving only his garment, a linen cloth, in their hands.

Jesus was taken away to confront the high priest with his assembly of all the chief priests, elders and scribes, and Peter followed at a distance right up to the high priest's palace and sat down with the servants by the fire. The chief priests and all the council looked vainly for witnesses for an excuse to put Jesus to death, for the witnesses they did find gave conflicting evidence. The high priest therefore challenged Jesus directly to reply, but at first He made no reply. When the high priest asked however if He were the Christ, Jesus replied that He was and announced His future station openly, whereat the high priest rent his clothes and dispensed with further evidence in the light of the ' blasphemy ', so that all condemned Jesus as guilty of death. Some then spat on Jesus, struck Him and mocked Him. Meanwhile Peter was challenged by the maids and others near him as being a Galilean by accent and therefore acquainted with Jesus. Three times Peter was challenged and each time he denied the challenge; the cock then crowed twice and he recalled Jesus' words and wept (14).

In the morning the chief priests, elders and scribes and the whole council consulted together, had Jesus bound and brought before Pilate who asked Him directly if He claimed to be the King of the Jews. Jesus acknowledged He was but made no further reply to other accusations. Pilate reminded them that at the passover, according to custom, he always released one prisoner of their choice and asked if they wanted the King of the Jews or Barabbas, a murderer caught in a recent popular rising. But the chief priests urged that they should choose Barabbas. Pilate then asked what he should do with the King of the Jews, and they replied to crucify him. So Barabbas was released and Jesus taken away for scourging and crucifixion. The escort of soldiers dressed Jesus up in purple, put a crown of thorns on His head, mockingly saluted Him, struck Him, spat on Him and bowed to Him. When they had had their fun they re-clothed Him in His own clothes and took Him off to crucify Him, compelling Simon of Cyrene, father of Alexander and Rufus, who had come in from the country, to carry the cross. They took Him out to Golgotha, offered Him a pain-killing drink of myrrh and wine which He refused, crucified Him and cast lots for His clothes. The crucifixion took place at about nine o'clock and a rough board with the words ' The King of the Jews ' was nailed above His head. On either side two thieves were crucified at the same time; passers-by and the chief priests and scribes who came to gloat, and His fellow sufferers also mocked Him for His ' blasphemous ' words and present helplessness. At noon there came a darkness over the land which lasted three hours until three o'clock when Jesus cried out " My God, my God, how thou has glorified me!" and died, ignoring an offer of a drink from a sponge with vinegar. The veil of the temple split in two from top to bottom. A centurion near the cross acknowledged from His bearing that Jesus was really the Son of God. Several women, including Mary of Magdala and Mary mother of James the less, of Joses and Salome, who had been with Jesus in Galilee and others who had accompanied Him to Jerusalem, stood watching at a distance.

At evening and because the next day was the Sabbath, Joseph of Arimathea, a counsellor of repute, was granted his request to be allowed to bury the body, and when Pilate had satisfied himself that Jesus was indeed dead, Joseph took the body down, wrapped it in fine linen cloth, placed it in a rock tomb and rolled a stone in front of the entrance. Mary of Magdala and Mary, mother of Joses, saw where the tomb was (15).

After the sabbath was over, Mary of Magdala and Mary, mother of James and Salome, went very early in the morning with sweet spices they had bought to anoint the body and arrived at the tomb at sunrise wondering how they could get past the large stone in front of the entrance. When they got there they saw the stone had already been rolled away; they were addressed in the tomb by a young man dressed in white who told them that Jesus had risen and gone and that they were to inform Peter and the disciples that He had departed for Galilee where He would see them. The women fled from the tomb, scared and amazed. Now Jesus first appeared to Mary of Magdala and she told His disciples as they were mourning, but they did not believe her. Jesus then appeared to two as they were walking in the country, and to the eleven disciples while they were eating and rebuked them for their scepticism and incredulity. He then commanded them to go out and preach the gospel to all men everywhere in the world, baptising those that responded with belief, and promising that those who believed would be able to cast out devils, speak with new tongues, take up serpents, be immune to poison and heal the sick. Jesus then ceased to appear to them but they went out preaching everywhere ' the Lord working with them and confirming the words with signs following '. (16).

(The numbers in brackets in this section refer to chapters of the Gospel)

Appendix B

JOHN'S GOSPEL

The principal events recorded in the Gospel of John may be briefly summarised as follows:

After baptism by John the Baptist, Jesus called His first three disciples (Andrew, Simon Peter and Philip) to follow Him and talked with Nathaniel (1). He attended a wedding at Cana in Galilee at which He turned water into wine, He visited Capernaum and went for the Passover to Jerusalem where He expelled traffickers from the Temple (2). He was visited by Nicodemus, a Pharisee, by night and answered his questions about His own mission, its purpose and the response to it (3). Jesus then travelled in Judaea with His disciples and made towards Galilee again going through Samaria on the way. In the vicinity of Samaria, Jesus held a long conversation with a Samaritan woman of easy virtue and finding her responsive announced to her His claim to be the Messiah. He stayed on in the area for two days as the Samaritans were receptive to His message and hospitable, and then proceeded on to Galilee. At Cana He met a nobleman from Capernaum at whose request He healed his son whom he had left sick at home (4). Jesus again went up to Jerusalem at the time of a Jewish feast and healed a man beside the pool of Bethesda who had been ill for 38 years. Because this healing took place on the Sabbath, when all work was prohibited, the Jews were offended and sought to kill Him. In response to Jewish criticisms Jesus explained His relationship with God as that of the Son with the Father, the spiritual identity of His message with that of Moses (5). Jesus then crossed the sea of Galilee followed by a crowd of about 5,000 people whom He fed with five loaves and two small fishes. After the meal the disciples filled twelve baskets with the fragments of food left over. Jesus withdrew Himself and the disciples recrossed the sea of Galilee to Capernaum. They ran into a storm but were joined by Jesus walking on the sea. The people sought out Jesus again and in answer to their questions He told them what they should put first in life, expounded the meaning of the " bread from heaven ", claimed Himself to be sent by God as the " bread of life " and in answer to critical comment reiterated His claim but averred twice that the Father must attract before any can recognise Him. He made it clear that it was the spirit that gave life, the flesh was of no value. Many therefore were disappointed and left Jesus. Peter acclaimed Him as the Anointed One, Son of the living God, and Jesus mentioned that one of His own twelve disciples was ' a devil ' (6). Jesus then travelled about Galilee for some time. He had an altercation with His brothers, who at the time did not believe in Him, over going openly to Jerusalem for the feast of tabernacles: they went and He followed secretly, but taught openly in the Temple where He replied to critics and had His first clash with the Pharisees who however refrained from action against Him because their officers were impressed and also because Nicodemus maintained that He should be heard before being judged (7). Next day Jesus was at the Temple again when He confuted the Pharisees, over the question of punishment for an adulteress, by challenging their hypocrisy. There followed further interchange with the Pharisees who challenged His claims and His authority, but could make no headway in their attempts to refute Him. As a result many hearers were drawn to Him but could not accept either His challenge or His claim to priority to Abraham (8). Jesus healed a man that had been blind from birth on the sabbath and again the Pharisees reacted when they heard of it by rejecting the man who therefore turned to Jesus and acknowledged Him (9). Jesus told the parable of the door and the good shepherd, and again at the Temple claimed the authority of the Son of God. Again He foiled an attempt to take Him and departed across Jordan (10). Jesus visited Bethany and at the request of Martha and Mary brought their brother Lazarus back to life after he had been dead four days. The Pharisees and chief priests, especially the high priest Caiaphas, got to hear about this, feared for their position and decided to put Him to death. Jesus departed to Ephraim (11). As the Passover approached Jesus returned via Bethany where Mary anointed His feet at table in spite of a protest from Judas Iscariot. He went up to Jerusalem on an ass and was hailed by many people who however failed to respond to Jesus' challenge to follow Him when such action meant sacrifice even to death (12). After supper, on the eve of the Passover, Jesus washed the feet of His disciples, explained the reason, singled out Judas Iscariot to consummate his intention, commanded the remaining disciples to love one another and warned Peter of his impending denials (13). In His last conversation with His disciples, after supper, Jesus spoke of the many mansions of His Father's house, of His own relationship with the Father, of His special commandment to them to love one another, of the Comforter, of His peace that He left with them (14). He strengthened His special commandment with the parable of the vine and indicated the effect of obedience (15), He warned them of the trials they would face and spoke again of the coming of the Comforter, announced that He was going to His Father (16). Jesus prayed extolling His Father and the station He had given Him, and for His disciples solemnising the purpose of His mission to raise up those who believed and followed and to establish and maintain their unity (17). Jesus went out with His disciples over Cedron into the garden where Judas conducted a band of men from the chief priest and Pharisees. Jesus was arrested after a scuffle in which Peter cut off a man's ear which Jesus healed, and was taken to Annas and then to Caiaphas and later to Pilate who interrogated Him but found no fault. When Pilate offered to release Him, Barabbas was demanded. Peter denied acquaintance with Jesus three times before the cock crew (18). Pilate had Jesus scourged and his soldiers mocked Him, but when Pilate tried to have Him released the chief priests insisted on His crucifixion for blasphemy. After a second interrogation and because the Jews insisted, Pilate handed Him over for crucifixion on Golgotha. The soldiers diced for His clothes. Jesus, crucified with two others in the presence of His mother, His aunt and Mary Magdalene and some disciples, asked John to look after His mother, and died. Joseph of Arimathea, a believer, obtained permission from Pilate to take the body of Jesus which with Nicodemus he wrapped in spices and put in a new rock tomb in a garden near Golgotha (19). Early on the day after the Sabbath Mary Magdalene visited the rock tomb, saw the stone rolled away, reported to the disciples two of whom ran up to investigate and found the body gone but the clothes lying there. Mary grief-stricken saw and heard two angels at the tomb and then became aware of Jesus Himself in the garden and conversed with Him. She reported this to the disciples. In the evening the disciples too experienced the presence of Jesus Who conversed with them, especially with Thomas, and strengthened their faith (20). The presence of Jesus was experienced for the third time by seven of the disciples when they were fishing. The disciples, who had caught nothing to eat, took advice from Jesus to try the other side of the boat and caught 153 fish. They then had a meal of bread and fish with Jesus Who expressly enjoined Peter three times to feed His sheep. Peter and another disciple were also adjured to to follow Jesus (21).

(*The numbers in brackets in this section refer to the chapters of the Gospel*)

Appendix C

PURPOSES OF JESUS AS STATED BY HIMSELF

Mark

1:17	" Come ye after me, and I will make you to become fishers of men "[1]
1:38	" Let us go into the next towns, that I may preach there also: for therefore came I forth "[2]
2:10	" The Son of man hath power on earth to forgive sins "[4]
2:17	" I came not to call the righteous, but sinners to repentance "[3]
2:28	" The Son of man is Lord also of the Sabbath "[5]
4:3	" Behold, there went out a sower to sow . . ."[2]
9:12	" It is written of the Son of man, that he must suffer many things, and be set at nought "[6]
10:33	" and the Son of man shall be delivered unto the chief priests, and unto the scribes . . ."[6]
10:45	" the Son of man came not to be ministered unto, but to minister, and to give his life a ransom for many "[7]
14:21	" The Son of man indeed goeth as it is written of him "[8]

Matthew

3:15	" thus it becometh us to fulfil all righteousness "[8]
4:17	" Repent, for the kingdom of heaven is at hand "[9]
4:19	" Follow me, and I will make you fishers of men "[1]
5:17	" Think not that I am come to destroy the law or the prophets: I am come not to destroy, but to fulfil "[3]
9:6	" the Son of man hath power on earth to forgive sins "[4]
9:13	" I am come not to call the righteous, but sinners to repentance "[3]
10:16	" I send you forth as sheep in the midst of wolves "[10]
10:34	" Think not that I am come to send peace on earth: I came not to send peace, but a sword. For I am come to set a man at variance against his father, and the daughter against her mother, and the daughter in law against her mother in law "[11]
11:27	" All things are delivered unto me of my Father: and no man knoweth the Son but the Father; neither knoweth any man the Father, save the Son, and he to whomsoever the Son will reveal him "[12]
11:28	" Come unto me, all ye that labour and are heavy laden, and I will give you rest. Take my yoke upon you, and learn of me; for I am meek and lowly in heart: and ye shall find rest unto your souls "[10]
12:8	" For the Son of man is Lord even of the sabbath day "[5]
12:28	" But if I cast our devils by the Spirit of God, then the kingdom of God is come unto you "[9]
12:30	" He that is not with me is against me; and he that gathereth not with me scattereth abroad "[11]
12:39	" there shall no sign be given to it, but the sign of the prophet Jonas " cf. 16:4[13]
12:50	" Whosoever shall do the will of my Father which is in heaven, the same is my brother and my sister and my mother "[10]
13:13-15	" Therefore speak I to them in parables: because they seeing see not; and hearing they hear not, neither do they understand "[14]
13:37-43	" He that soweth the good seed is the Son of man; the field is the world . . ."[2]
15:24	" I am not sent but unto the lost sheep of the house of Israel "[16]
16:11	" How is it that ye do not understand that I spake it not to you concerning bread, that ye should beware of the leaven of the Pharisees and of the Sadducees?"[15]
18:11	" For the Son of man is come to save that which was lost "[3]

114

20:28	" Even as the Son of man came not to be ministered unto, but to minister, and to give his life a ransom for many "[7]
23:37	" O Jerusalem . . . how often would I have gathered thy children together . . ."[16] & [2]
26:28	" For this is my blood of the new testament, which is shed for many for the remission of sins "[18]

Luke

2:49	" Wist ye not that I must be about my Father's business?"[10]
4:18-19	" The Spirit of the Lord is upon me, because he hath anointed me to preach the gospel to the poor; he hath sent me to heal the broken-hearted, to preach deliverance to the captives, and recovering of sight to the blind, to set at liberty them that are bruised, to preach the acceptable year of the Lord "[17] & [3]
4:43	" I must preach the kingdom of God to other cities also: for therefore am I sent "[2]
5:24	" the Son of man hath power on earth to forgive sins "[4]
5:32	" I came not to call the righteous, but sinners to repentance "[3]
6:5	" the Son of man is Lord also of the sabbath "[5]
9:22	" The Son of man must suffer many things, and be rejected of the elders and chief priests and scribes, and be slain, and be raised the third day "[6]
9:56	" For the Son of man is not come to destroy men's lives, but to save them "[3]
11:23	" He that is not with me is against me: and he that gathereth not with me scattereth "[11]
12:49	" I am come to send fire on earth: and what will I, if it be already enkindled?"[11]
12:51	" Suppose ye that I am come to give peace on earth? I tell you, Nay; but rather division "[11]
13:34	" O Jerusalem . . .How often would I have gathered thy children together, as a hen doth gather her brood under her wings, and ye would not!" [16] & [10]
19:10	" For the Son of man is come to seek and to save that which was lost "[3]
22:19	" This is my body which is given for you: this do in remembrance of me "[18]
22:37	" . . . this that is written must yet be accomplished in me, And he was reckoned among the transgressors . . ."[8]
24:44	" These are the words which I spake unto you, while I was yet with you, that all things must be fulfilled, which were written in the law of Moses, and in the prophets, and in the psalms, concerning me "[8]
24:46-47	" Thus it is written, and thus it behoved Christ to suffer, and to rise from the dead the third day: and that repentance and remission of sins should be preached in his name among all nations, beginning at Jerusalem "[8] & [16] & [2]

John

3:14-15	" And as Moses lifted up the serpent in the wilderness, even so must the Son of man be lifted up, that whosoever believeth in him should not perish, but have eternal life. For God so loved the world, that he sent his only begotten Son, that whosoever believeth in him should not perish but have everlasting life. For God sent not his Son into the world to condemn the world; but that the world through him might be saved "[3] & [4]
4:34	" My meat is to do the will of him that sent me, and to finish his work "[8] and [10] and [12]
5:30	" I can of my own self do nothing: as I hear, I judge: and my judgment is just; because I seek not mine own will, but the will of the Father which hath sent me "[12]

115

5:36	" But I have greater witness than that of John: for the works which the Father hath given me to finish, the same works that I do. bear witness of me, that the Father hath sent me "[11] & [12]
6:38-40	" For I came down from heaven, not to do mine own will, but the will of him that sent me. And this is the Father's will which hath sent me, that of all which he hath given me I should lose nothing, but should raise it up again at the last day. And this is the will of him that sent me, that every one which seeth the Son, and believeth on him, may have everlasting life: and I will raise him up at the last day "[4] & [12]
6:50-51	" This is the bread which cometh down from heaven, that a man may eat therof and not die. I am the living bread which came down from heaven: if any man eat of this bread, he shall live for ever: and the bread that I will give is my flesh, which I will give for the life of the world "[4]
7:16-17	" My doctrine is not mine, but his that sent me. If any man will do his will, he shall know of the doctrine, whether it be of God, or whether I speak of myself "[10] & [12]
8:26	" I have many things to say and to judge of you: but he that sent me is true; and I speak to the world those things which I have heard of him "[11] & [12]
8:28-29	" When ye have lifted up the Son of man, then ye shall know that I am he, and that I do nothing of myself; but as my Father hath taught me, I speak these things. And he that sent me is with me: the Father hath not left me alone; for I do always those things that please him "[12] & [13]
8:42	" If God were your Father, ye would love me: for I proceeded forth and came from God; neither came I of myself, but he sent me "[12]
8:50	" And I seek not my own glory: there is one that seeketh and judgeth "[12]
9:4-5	" I must work the works of him that sent me, while it is day: the night cometh, when no man can work. So long as I am in the world, I am the light of the world "[12]
9:39	" For judgment I am come into this world, that they which see not might see, and that they which see might be made blind "[11]
10:7-11	" . . . I am the door of the sheep . . . I am come that they might have life, and that they might have it more abundantly . . . I am the good shepherd : the good shepherd giveth his life for the sheep "[4] & [10]
12:27	" Now is my soul troubled; and what shall I say? Father, save me from this hour: but for this cause came I unto this hour "[6]
12:46-47	" I am come a light into the world, that whosoever believeth on me should not abide in darkness. And if any man hear my words, and believe not, I judge him not: for I came not to judge the world, but to save the world "[3] & [10]
13:15	" For I have given you an example, that ye should do as I have done to you "[10]
13:19	" Now I tell you before it come, that, when it is come to pass, ye may believe that I am he "[13]
14:3	" And if I go and prepare a place for you, I will come again, and receive you unto myself ; that where I am, there ye may be also "[13] & [10]
14:5	" I am the way, the truth, and the life: no man cometh unto the Father, but by me "[10]
14:15	" If ye love me, keep my commandments "[10]
14:29	" And now I have told you before it came to pass, that, when it is come to pass, ye might believe "[13]
14:31	" But that the world may know that I love the Father; and as the Father gave me commandment, even so I do "[12]

15:12   " This is my commandment, that ye love one another, even as I have loved you "[10]

15:16-17   " Ye have not chosen me, but I have chosen you, and ordained you, that ye should go and bring forth fruit, and that your fruit should remain: that whatsoever ye shall ask of the Father in my name, he may give it you. These things I command you, that ye love one another "[10]

16:1   " These things I have spoken unto you, that ye should not be offended "[13]

16:4   " But these things I have told you, that when the time shall come, ye may remember that I told you of them "[13]

16:33   " These things I have spoken unto you, that in me ye might have peace "[10]

17:2   " As thou hast given him power over all flesh, that he should give eternal life to as many as thou hast given him "[4]

17-20-26   " . . . that they all may be one; as thou, Father art in me, and I in thee, that they also may be one in us: that the world may believe that thou hast sent me. And the glory which thou gavest me I have given them; that they may be one, even as we are one: I in them, and thou in me, that they may be made perfect in one; and that the world may know that thou hast sent me, and hast loved them, as thou hast loved me. Father, I will that they also, whom thou hast given me, be with me where I am; that they may behold my glory, which thou hast given me: for thou lovedst me before the foundation of the world. O righteous Father, the world hath not known thee: but I have known thee, and these have known that thou hast sent me. And I have declared unto them thy name, and will declare it: that the love wherewith thou hast loved me may be in them, and I in them "[19]

18:37   " To this end was I born, and for this cause came I into the world, that I should bear witness unto the truth "[8]

20:21   " Peace be unto you: as my Father hath sent me, even so send I you "[10] & [12] & [19]

117

Appendix D

THE PARABLES OF JESUS

Note: the numbers indicate the order of reference and use in Chapter 8

Mark

4:3-20	The sower and the word[1]
4:21-22	Candle to be set on a candlestick[2]
4:26-29	Kingdom of God as a seed[38]
4:30-32	Kingdom of God as a grain of mustard seed[40]
12:1-11	The vineyard[43]
13:28	The figtree putting forth leaves[65]
13:34	The Son of man as a man journeying[41]

Matthew

5:13	Ye are the salt of the earth[4]
5:14	Ye are the light of the world[3]
5:29-30	And if thy right eye offend thee . . .[20]
6:19-21	Lay not up for yourselves treasure upon earth . . .[8]
6:22-23	The light of the body is the eye . . .[7]
7:3-5	The mote and the beam[9]
7:13-14	Enter ye in at the strait gate . . .[57]
7:15-20	Beware of false prophets . . . by their fruits ye shall know them . . .[60]
7:24-27	House built on rock or sand[10]
9:15	Can the children of the bridechamber mourn . . .[11]
9:16	New cloth and old garments[15]
9:17	New wine and old bottles[16]
9:37-38	Harvest plenteous, labourers few[18]
10:16	As sheep in the midst of wolves[14]
11:16	This generation like children sitting in the markets[37]
12:43-45	The unclean spirit and the seven other spirits[22]
13:3-23	The sower and the word[1]
13:24-43	Kingdom of heaven: the wheat and the tares[42]
13:31-32	Kingdom of heaven like a grain of mustard seed[40]
13:33	Kingdom of heaven like leaven[39]
13:44	Kingdom of heaven like a treasure hid in a field[55]
13:45	Kingdom of heaven like a merchant seeking goodly pearls[56]
13:47-50	Kingdom of heaven like a net[46]
13:52	Every scribe instructed unto the kingdom of heaven as a householder[45]
15:11-20	That which cometh out of the mouth defileth a man[21]
18:11-14	The one lost sheep[5]
18:23-35	Kingdom of heaven like a king and his harvests[44]
19:11-12	Eunuchs[13]
19:23-24	Camel and the needle's eye[28] [50]
20:1-16	Kingdom of heaven: labourers and householder's vineyard[47]
21:27-31	The two sons, willing and unwilling[12]
21:33-41	The vineyard[43]
21:42-44	The stone rejected by the builders[24]
22:2-14	Kingdom of heaven: the king's son's wedding[48]
24:32-33	The figtree putting forth leaves[65]
24:45-51	The faithful servant and the evil servant[52]
25:1-12	The wise and the foolish virgins[51]
25:14-30	Kingdom of heaven: The servants and the talents[53]

Appendix E

THE MIRACLES OF JESUS

Mark

1:23-27	Healing man with unclean spirit in synagogue at Capernaum
1:30-31	Healing Simon's wife's mother of a fever
1:40-45	Cleansing of a leper in Galilee
2:3-12	Healing man sick of the palsy
3:1-5	Healing man with withered hand on a sabbath
4:37-41	Calming the storm
5:2-20	Casting out unclean spirit in Gadara
5:22-43	Raising the daughter of Jairus, ruler of the synagogue
5:25-34	Healing woman of issue of blood
6:33-44	Feeding the 5,000 in a desert place
6:47-51	Walking on the sea of Galilee
7:25-30	Casting out devil from daughter of Syrophenician Greek woman
7:32-37	Healing deaf and dumb man by the sea of Galilee
8:1-9	Feeding the 4,000
8:22-26	Healing the blind man at Bethsaida
9:16-29	Casting out deaf and dumb spirit from boy
10:46-52	Healing blind Bartimaeus by Jericho
11:13-21	Cursing the figtree
16:9-14	Appearances of Jesus after the crucifixion

John

2:1-11	Turning water into wine at the marriage feast of Cana
4:46-54	Healing the son of a nobleman of Capernaum, of a fever at a distance
5:2-17	Healing the impotent man (sick for 38 years) beside the pool of Bethseda at Jerusalem on a sabbath
6:2-14	Feeding the 5,000 on the mountain by the sea of Galilee
6:16-21	Walking on the sea
9:1-41	Healing the man blind from birth on the sabbath
11:1-46	Raising of Lazarus from the tomb at Bethany, after 4 days
20:11-31	Appearances of Jesus after the crucifixion
21:4-22	More appearances of Jesus; the great catch of 153 fishes

Matthew

8:2-4	Cleansing the leper in Galilee
8:5-13	Healing the centurion's servant of the palsy
8:14-15	Healing Peter's mother in law of fever
8:24-27	Calming the storm on the sea of Galilee
8:28-33	Casting out devils from two in the country of the Gergesenes and the herd of swine
9:2-8	Healing man sick of the palsy
9:18-25	Raising the ruler's daughter
9:20-22	Healing woman of issue of blood
9:27-31	Restoring sight of two blind men
9:32-33	Casting out devil from dumb man
12:10-13	Healing man with withered hand in the synagogue on the sabbath
12:22-23	Healing of blind and dumb man
14:13-21	Feeding the 5,000 in a desert place with 5 loaves and 2 fishes
14:24-33	Walking on the water (also Peter)
15:22-28	Healing of woman of Canaan's daughter of a devil, near Tyre
15:32-38	Feeding the 4,000 near Galilee with 7 loaves and a few fishes
17:1-9	Transfiguration on Mt. Tabor, with Moses and Elias
17:14-21	Casting out devil from lunatic boy

120

17:24-27	Piece of money for tribute from mouth of fish
20:30-34	Restoring sight to two blind men near Jericho
21:18-21	Cursing the figtree near Jerusalem
28:9-20	Appearances of Jesus after the crucifixion

Luke

4:33-36	Casting out devil from man in synagogue in Capernaum on the sabbath
4:38-39	Healing Simon's mother in law of a fever
5:3-11	The large draught of fishes
5:12-14	Cleansing a leper
5:18-25	Healing man with a palsy
6:6-10	Healing man with withered hand in the synagogue on the sabbath
7:2-10	Healing centurion's sick servant, at a distance, at Capernaum
7:12-16	Raising only son of a widow at Nain
8:22-25	Calming the storm
8:27-39	Casting out legion of devils from man in Gadara into the herd of swine
8:41-56	Raising of daughter of Jairus, ruler of synagogue
8:43-48	Healing woman of issue of blood
9:11-17	Feeding the 5,000 in a desert place with 5 loaves and 2 fishes
9:28-37	Transfiguration on the mountain, with Moses and Elias
9:38-42	Casting out of unclean spirit from child
13:10-17	Healing woman of spirit of infirmity (18 years) in the synagogue on the sabbath
14:1-6	Healing man of dropsy in house of a Pharisee on the sabbath
17:12-19	Cleansing ten lepers, one grateful
18:35-43	Restoring sight of blind man near Jericho
22:49-57	Healing ear of priest's servant cut off by sword
24:15-51	Appearances of Jesus after crucifixion

Appendix F

NOTES AND REFERENCES

Foreword
1. John 10:7
2. John 10:1

Chapter I—The Life of Jesus
1. " Prayers and Meditations " by Bahá'u'lláh, translated by Shoghi Effendi, 1938 edition pp. 112-113
2. Matthew 16:17
3. Matthew 26:46. This passage, " My God, my God, why hast Thou forsaken me?" is clearly erroneous: the link between Christ the Son and God the Father is of a kind that could never be broken. The best explanation lies in supposing that " some of them that stood there " misheard or misquoted a cry which, with very slight change, can be translated as, " My God, my God, how Thou hast glorified me!"
4. "Will and Testament of ' Abdu'l-Bahá " translated by Shoghi Effendi, published in " Covenant of Bahá'u'lláh " 1963 edition pp. 98-99
5. "Gleanings from the Writings of Bahá'u'lláh" translated by Shoghi Effendi 1949 edition p. 85

Chapter II—Interpretation of Scripture
1. John 8:12
2. John 9:5
3. John 12:46
4. John 3:13
5. John 3:6
6. Matthew 26:41
7. John 9:39
8. John 9:41
9. John 15:22
10. Matthew 15:14 cf. Luke 6:39
11. Mark 4:9, 4:23, 7:16, Matthew 11:15, 13:9, 13:43, Luke 8:8
12. John 6:63
13. Mark 13:31, Matthew 24:35, Luke 21:33

Chapter III—Some Problems
1. Mark 14:30
2. John 13:38
3. John 14:16, 26, 15:26, 16:7
4. John 14:3, 14:28, cf. Revelations 3:11, 3:22, 7:12, 22:21
5. John 16:13
6. John 21:15-17
7. Mark 13:35
8. Mark 13:33, 13:35, 13:37
9. Mark 14:38, Matthew 26:41
10. John 1:1
11. John 8:58
12. John 14:28
13. John 16:7
14. John 16-12-13.
15. John 10:16
16. John 14:6
17. Mark 16:23
18. Mark 6:45
19. Matthew 7:16

122

Chapter IV—What Jesus did not teach

1. Matthew 15:9
2. Matthew 11:19
3. Matthew 6:16-18
4. Luke 12:31
5. Mark 7:15, 18
6. Matthew 18:3
7. Matthew 8:20, Luke 9:58
8. Luke 20:34-35
9. Matthew 19:4
10. John 15:22-24
11. Mark 12:26-27 cf. Matthew 22:31-32
12. John 5:46
13. John 3:6
14. Matthew 16:16
15. Matthew 16:18-19
16. John 14:6-7
17. John 14:9, 11
18. John 15:16
19. Luke 14:23
20. Matthew 28:18-20
21. Matthew 24:35, Mark 13:31, Luke 21:33
22. John 17:18-24
23. Matthew 26:26, Mark 14:22, cf. Luke 22:19
24. Matthew 26:27-28, cf. Mark 14:24, Luke 22:20
25. Matthew, 19:26, cf. Mark 10:27
26. Matthew 22:42-44
27. Matthew 22:45
28. Matthew 16:16
29. Matthew 26:63-64
30. Matthew 27:11
31. Luke 3-23, 4:22, John 1:45, 6:42
32. Genesis 17:17
33. Genesis 21:1-2
34. Luke 1:5-25, 36
35. Isaiah 7:14
36. Luke 1:26-35
37. Matthew 19:17, Mark 10:18
38. Mark 13:32
39. Matthew 21:33-40, Mark 12:1-9, Luke 20:9-16
40. John 14:28
41. John 16:26
42. John 16:28
43. John 8:28
44. Luke 4:24
45. Matthew 13:57, Mark 6:4
46. e.g. Matthew 10:40, Mark 9:37, Luke 9:48, John 4:34, 5:23, etc.
47. Luke 4:43
48. John 4:34
49. Luke 3:16
50. Mark 7:15-16
51. Matthew 15:17-20
52. Matthew 12:33, 35
53. Matthew 6:19-21
54. Luke 9:60 cf. Matthew 8:22
55. John 10:10
56. John 12:24-26
57. John 5:39-40
58. John 17:3
59. Luke 6:29

60. Matthew 5:39
61. Matthew 10:34
62. Mark 11:15-18
63. Luke 14:23
64. Matthew 10:21-22
65. Matthew 26:52
66. Matthew 7:19, Luke 6:43
67. Mark 3:31-32, John 7:3, 5, 10, Matthew 13:55
68. John 2:4
69. Mark 3:33-35
70. John 19:26-27
71. Matthew 1:19
72. Luke 2:49
73. John 2:3-4
74. Mark 9:50
75. Matthew 10:24
76. Mark 10:42-45
77. Luke 12:1
78. Matthew 16:6, 11
79. Mark 8:15
80. Mark 23:9
81. Mark 12:1-11, Matthew 21:33-40, Luke 20:9-16
82. Mark 7:7
83. Matthew 3:11, Luke 3:16

Chapter V—Neglected teachings of Christ

1. John 1:12-13
2. Genesis 2:7
3. Genesis 17:17, 21:1-2
4. Luke 1:5-25, 26
5. John 1:45, 6:42, Luke 3:43, 4:22
6. Matthew 22:42-45, Mark 12:35-37, Luke 20:41-44
7. John 6:50
8. Luke 23:43
9. John 3:13
10. John 3:6
11. Isaiah 40:7-8
12. Luke 12:28, I Peter 1:24-25
13. John 13:34-35
14. Matthew 18:3
15. Matthew 7:21
16. Matthew 5:19
17. Matthew 26:52
18. Luke 6:27-28, Matthew 5:44
19. Mark 2:27
20. Mark 12:38-39
21. Matthew 21:19

Chapter VI—What did Jesus teach?

1. Mark 1:17, cf. Matthew 4:10
2. Matthew 13:37-38
3. Luke 4:43, cf. Matthew 13:37-43, 23:37, Mark 1:38, Luke 13:34, 24:46-47
4. Luke 19:10, cf. Matthew 5:17, 9:13, 18:11, Mark 2:17, Luke 4:18-19, 5:32, 9:56, John 3:14-15, 12:46-50
5. John 3:14-15, cf. Matthew 9:6, Mark 2:10, Luke 5:24, John 6:38-39, 50:51, 10:7-11, 17:2
6. Matthew 12:8, cf. Mark 2:28, Luke 6:5
7. Luke 9:22, cf. Mark 9:12, 10:33, John 12:27
8. Mark 10:45, cf. Matthew 20:28
9. Mark 14:21, cf. Matthew 3:15, Luke 22:37, 24:44, 46:47, John 18:37

10. Matthew 12:28, cf. Matthew 4:17
11. John 15:16-17, cf. Matthew 10:16, 11:28, 12:50, Luke 21:49, John 4:34, 7:16-17, 10:7-11, 12:46-50, 13:15, 14:3, 14:6, 14:15, 15:12, 16:33, 20:21
12. Matthew 10:34, cf. Matthew 12:30, Luke 11:23, 12:49, 12:51, John 5:36, 8:26, 9:39
13. John 8:28-29, cf. Matthew 11:87, John 4:34, 5:30, 5:36, 7:16-17, 8:26. 8:42, 8:50, 9:4-5, 14:31, 20:21
14. John 13:19, cf. Matthew 12:39, John 8:27-29, 14:3, 14:29, 16:1, 16:4
15. Matthew 13:13-15
16. Matthew 16:11, cf. Mark 8:15
17. Luke 24:46-47, cf. Matthew 15:24, 23:37, Luke 13:34
18. Luke 4:18-19
19. Matthew 26:28, cf. Luke 23:19
20. John 17:20-26, cf. John 20:21

Chapter VII—Review of the Gospels

1. John 1:43, 12:26, 21:22, Mark 2:14, 8:34, 10:21, Matthew 4:19, 8:22, 9:9, 16:24, 19:21, Luke 5:27, 9:23, 9:59, 18:22
2. John 8:11, 8:42-47, 15:22-24
3. John 14:1, 14:27
4. John 14:15, 15:4, 15:9, 15:12, 15:17
5. John 3:17, 4:34, 5:17, 5:19-23, 5:26-27, 5:30, 5:36-37, 5:43, etc.
6. John 8:51, 14:21, 15:14
7. John 15:7, 15:10
8. John 13:4-16
9. John 21:16, 21:17
10 John 1:43, 8:12, 12:26
11. Mark 4:24, 7:14, 8:15-2, 13:5, 13:9, 13:23, 3:33
12. Mark 13:33, 13:35, 13:37, 14:34, 14:38
13. Mark 1:17, 2:14, 8:39
14. Mark 13:13, 13:33, 14:38
15. Mark 1:15, 5:36, 11:22
16. Mark 9:43, 9:45, 9:47

Chapter VIII—Parables

1. Matthew 13:3-23, Mark 4:3-20, Luke 8:5-15
2. Matthew 5:13
3. Mark 4:34
4. John 2:19

Chapter IX—Miracles

1. Mark 1:44
2. Matthew 4:4
3. Matthew 12:39, 16:4
4. John 9:39
5. Matthew 4:23-24, 8:16-17, 9:35, 10:1, 14:36, 15:30-31, 19:2, 21:14, Mark 1:34, 1:39, 3:10-12, 3:15, 3:22, 3:23-30, 6:5, 6:13, 6:55-56, 9:38-40, Luke 4:40-41, 5:15, 6:17-19, 7:21, 9:1-2, 9:11, 11:14-15, John 2:23, 3:2, 7:31, 12:37
6. Mark 2:3-12, 2:17, John 5:14-15, 9:24
7. Matthew 12:31, Mark 3:23-29
8. Matthew 13:14-15, John 12:40
9. Matthew 8:22
10. John 3:6

Chapter X—A Coherent Pattern

1. John 3:1-21
2. Mark 12:28-34
3. John 19:23-24
4. Luke 4:28-30

5. Mark 2:25-28, etc.
6. Exodus 24:8, Matthew 26:28
7. Deuteronomy 6:16, Luke 4:12
8. Psalm 35:19, 69:4, John 15:25
9. Psalm 41:9, John 13:18
10. Psalm 78:24, John 31-33
11. Psalm 109:7-8, John 17:12
12. Psalm 110:1, Matthew 22:42-45, Mark 12:35-37, Luke 20:41-44
13. Psalm 118:22, Luke 20:17
14. Isaiah 6:9-10, Matthew 13:14-15
15. Isaiah 29:13, Matthew 15:8-9
16. Isaiah 35:5, Matthew 11:5
17. Isaiah 54:13, John 6:45
18. Isaiah 53:12, Luke 22:37
19. Isaiah 61:1-2, Luke 4:18-19
20. Daniel 9:27, 12:11, Matthew 24:15, Mark 13:14
21. Micah 7:6, Matthew 10:35-36
22. Zechariah 13:7, Mark 14:27
23. Malachi 3:1, Matthew 11:10, Luke 7:27
24. Malachi 4:5-6, Matthew 17:10-12
25. John 18:36
26. Matthew 10:34
27. John 10:30
28. Mark 13:32
29. Mark 10:40
30. John 16:13
31. John 5:47
32. Matthew 12:8
33. Matthew 23:3
34. Luke 16:31, cf. Matthew 22:32
35. John 6:32-33
36. John 1:45, 5:46
37. John 3:14-16
38. Numbers 21:8
39. Mark 10:19, Luke 18:20
40. Exodus 20:2-3
41. Mark 12:29
42. Mark 12:30
43. Exodus 20:4-6
44. John 4:24
45. Exodus 20:7
46. Matthew 5:34, 37
47. Exodus 20:8-11
48. Matthew 2:28
49. Matthew 18:20
50. Exodus 20:12
51. Luke 18:20
52. Luke 2:49
53. Matthew 10:35
54. Matthew 19:5
55. Mark 7:10-13
56. Exodus 20:13
57. John 18:11
58. Matthew 26:52
59. Matthew 5:9
60. John 10:10
61. Luke 6:35-38
62. Exodus 20:14
63. Matthew 5:28
64. Exodus 20:15
65. Matthew 19:18-21

126

66. Matthew 6:20
67. Luke 12:34
68. Matthew 5:48
69. Exodus 20:16
70. Mark 12:31
71. Exodus 20:17
72. Mark 1:44
73. Leviticus ch. 14
74. Deuteronomy 4:44
75. Mark 7:10, (cf. Matthew 15:4), Exodus 20:12, 21:17
76. Mark 10:3-5, (cf. Matthew 19:8, 5:31), Deuteronomy 24:1
77. Mark 10:19, (cf. Matthew 19:18-19, Luke 18:20), Exodus ch. 20
78. Mark 12:26, (cf. Matthew 22:32, Luke 20:37), Exodus 3:2-6
79. Mark 12:29, (cf. Matthew 5:43, 19:19, 22:37-39, Luke 10:27-28), Deuteronomy 6:4-5, Leviticus 19:18
80. Matthew 4:4 (cf. Luke 4:4), Deuteronomy 8:3
81. Matthew 4:7 (cf. Luke 4:12), Deuteronomy 6:16
82. Matthew 4:10 (cf. Luke 4:8), Deuteronomy 6:13
83. Matthew 5:21, Exodus 20:13
84. Matthew 5:27, Exodus 20:14
85. Matthew 5:33, Deuteronomy 5:11, 23:23
86. Matthew 5:38, Exodus 21:24
87. Matthew 12:5, Numbers 28:9-10
88. Matthew 18:16, Deuteronomy 19:15
89. Matthew 26:28, Exodus 24:8
90. John 3:14, Numbers 21:8-9
91. Matthew 21:19, Mark 11:14
92. Mark 10:2-12, Matthew 19:3-12, 5:31-32, Luke 16:18
93. Mark 2:23-28, 3:2-5, Matthew 12:1-8, Luke 6:1-10, 13:10-17, 14:1-6, John 7:22-23
94. John 7:22-23, Acts 15:1-29
95. Acts 10:9-17, 10:28, 15:29

Chapter XI—Perspective and Reality

1. See " Hidden Words " by Bahá'u'lláh, translated by Shoghi Effendi
2. " Divine Philosophy " by Soraya Chamberlain, 1918, p. 15
3. Mark 12:29-31
4. 'Abdu'l-Bahá quoted in " Divine Philosophy " p. 31
5. Mark 12:26-27. Luke 20:38
6. Luke 16:19-31
7. Mark 9: 2-9, Matthew 17:1-9, Luke 9:28-36
8. Luke 23:43
9. " Bahá'i Revelation " 1955 p. 201
10. " Promulgation of Universal Peace " 1943, pp. 3-4
11. " Promulgation of Universal Peace " 1943, p. 207

Chapter XII—Progressive Revelation

1. " Thief in the Night " by William Sears, 1961, p. 70
2. I Peter 1:17, 13, 5:1, 4, II Peter 1:19, 3:3-4, 9-10, 12, James 5:7-8, I Corinthians 1:7, 4:5, 11:26, 15:23-24, Philemon 1:6, 3:20, etc.
3. Matthew 24:13-14
4. Luke 21:24-27
5. Matthew 24:15
6. Daniel 9:24-25
7. Daniel 8:13-14
8. Isaiah 11:11, Jeremiah 49:34-39, Daniel 8:2
9. Nabil's Narrative " The Dawn Breakers ", translated by Shoghi Effendi, 1932, p. 92
10. Revelations 11:14

11. "Bahá'i' Revelation" 1955, pp. 3-34, Bahá'u'lláh's Tablets to the Kings, also extensively quoted in "Promised Day is Come" by Shoghi Effendi, 1961
12. Matthew 21:40, Mark 12:9, Luke 20:15, John 16:13
13. Luke 12:39, Revelations 3:3, 16:15, cf. II Peter 3:10
14. Matthew 24:32, Mark 13:28, Luke 21:29-30
15. Matthew 7:15
16. Matthew 24:5, Mark 13:6
17. Matthew 13:24-30
18. Matthew 16:6-11, Luke 12:1, Mark 8:15
19. Matthew 24:22, Mark 13:20
20. John 14:16, 26, 15:26, 16:7
21. John 14:3, 14:28, cf. Revelations 3:11, 22:7, 12, 22:21
22. Matthew 21:40, Mark 12:9, Luke 20:15
23. John 16:13
24. Matthew 6:10, Luke 11:2
25. Matthew 24:35, Mark 13:31, Luke 21:33
26. "Gleanings from the Writings of Bahá'u'lláh" translated by Shoghi
27. Effendi, 1949 p. 85
     "Tablet of Ahmad" by Bahá'u'lláh
28. Genesis 18:18, 22:18, 26:4
29. From Sarah through Isaac were descended Moses and Joseph, husband of the Mother of Jesus
30. From Hagar through Ishmael descended Muhammad and Siyyid 'Ali Muhammad, the Báb
31. Genesis 25:1
32. Deuteronomy 18:21-22, Isaiah 55:11
33. Isaiah 11:1, 11:10
34. Isaiah 9:6-7
35. Matthew 4:19, Mark 1:17
36. Numerous passages e.g. John 4:34, 5:23-24, 12:44, 17:3, etc.
37. Mark 13:32, Matthew 24:36
38. Mark 1:12, Luke 22:42, John 13:16, 14:28
39. Matthew 19:17, Mark 10:18
40. John 18:36
41. John 14:27
42. Matthew 10:34
43. Matthew 16:27, Mark 8:38
44. "Promised Day is Come" by Shoghi Effendi 1961, p. 124
45. Isaiah 11:6, cf. Isaiah 65:25
46. Revelations 21:1, Isaiah 65:17
47. Revelations 21:2
48. Revelations 21:1, 4, cf. Isaiah 65-17
49. Isaiah 11:9
50. Matthew 6:10, Luke 11:2, cf. Matthew 25:34 ff.